OPERATION EMU

B. BRANDON BARKER

To Tammy!
Enjoy!
B. B̶r̶ B̶r̶

Shrouded Rock Press

Upperville

cover art and EMU logo by Craig LaRotonda,
Revelation Studios

printed and bound in the united states of america.
www.colorplant.com

ISBN # 0-9773763-3-8

The night grew darke and we hearde whooly tales of the war-weary tribe calld Ko-Man-Chay. And howe a brayve soldier killed his very owne brother and was banishd to a once forsaken lande far Northe. And ere the bitter morning journey on foote with his wives and his children, he hath borne a younge son which he held up to the pale sun and namd Mee-Maw, or Leftover Mulch.

--Journals of James Spenser Spayde, 1604

i.

Every Wednesday in the Dorothy Stratten Memorial Conference Room at Jeffries Studios, there's a pitch meeting. Attendees include film director Enoch Jeffries, assistant director Doniphan Smith and sometimes a casting director. Five subjects are scheduled – most often writers or producers with a movie concept – and each is given five minutes to present an idea. On occasion, subjects are invited back for further discussion. The studio options fifteen pitches a year; of those it may produce one.

On this typical Wednesday, Enoch Jeffries – a small, well-preserved black man with a slight spinal curvature that cocked his head to one side – parked his white '95 Lexus in the lot and went to the A/V room in Building C, one of four beige warehouses, to watch the dailies from *Asylum Angels 3: Parole Denied*, his most recent project and, he hoped, his very last low-budget movie ever. Soon, he would begin pre-production for *Slow Death*, his first multi-million dollar picture in the thirty years since he made *It Lived in the Bomb Shelter* with a Super-8 camera and six wads of Silly Putty. He had acquired the rights to *Slow Death,* based on the best-selling lacrosse adventure comic, after a hard-fought bidding war that involved several industry heavies. But it was Paramount Pictures' large capital offering that gave his studio the edge, as did the enthusiasm of a filmmaker who had, for better or worse, made over 300 audacious low-budget features since 1969 and who was now considered, in some desperate circles, a Hollywood legend.

Skimming through the Cell Inspection scene for *Asylum Angels 3*, he couldn't help but take pride in the fact that, only a year ago, he was still auditioning actresses by having them kick a punching bag in high-heels and jog around his swimming pool shooting blanks on a 10mm Glock Autopistol. That epic phase of his career was now over. Gone were the days of state-hopping in white cargo vans. Gone were the days of hauling fake blood in milk jugs and begging city council wonks for permission to film guerilla ambushes in old quarries or skinny-dipping scenes in public parks. With the Paramount name behind him, the *Slow Death* buzz, and, of course, big-name actors, he could ignore these marginal hurdles and allow more time to focus on The Creative.

He popped a Mountain Dew and fast-forwarded through the final seconds of "Cell Inspection" – the last of the Cell Block scenes before they went on location at Chowchilla for the prison yard brawls – and decided on Take One for its raw and unhurried charm, plus the fact that the sound worked and the boom didn't drop into the frame. For a B-grade, straight-to-DVD romantic thriller with a 500k budget, *Asylum Angels 3* looked decent. He made a quick note to cut the Tooth Extraction sequence in Scene 6, and checked the clock above the door: pitch meeting in ten minutes. He swiveled around and tossed the soda can at the big trashcan by the door. It missed and landed on the floor.

Assistant Director Doniphan Smith, a twenty-eight year-old kid in a trench coat, peeked in. "Sir?"

"Yeah?"

"You sound a little low."

"Well, look." Jeffries pointed at the can.

Doniphan picked it up, pump-faked and dunked it into the trash.

"Fuck you, Donnie," he said, pulling a white visor over his head.

"Fuck you, sir."

"Let's go to the fucking pitch meeting."

"Okay."

On his way out of the AV building, Jeffries stopped at the hall mirror. Before every shoot, every meeting, every confrontation with humanity, he stopped here. He patted his unkempt Afro, removed his glasses and blinked at his foggy reflection. Now that he had acquired *Slow Death,* his name would have a little more cachet. Therefore, he could expect at this pitch meeting, if not heavyweights, at least upper-middleweights with concepts beyond the usual desert-island nymphs, zero-gravity fornication and kung fu fighting in motel parking lots. From this day forward he would settle for nothing less than grand inspiration; stories about hospitals and underdog sports teams, unrequited love, unexplainable romantic madness, the superheroes inside us all. He put his glasses back on and whispered, "Let's party."

• • •

Jeffries breezed into the conference room.

"Nice lineup, Donnie." He waved the pitch agenda sheet.

"Please call me Doniphan, sir."

"Duly noted."

Cheryl, the associate producer/receptionist, peeked in.

"Ready, Mr. Jeffries?"

He raised his thumb.

"How were the dailies?"

] 3 [

"Like this…" Jeffries made an *OK* sign.

Cheryl returned with two blonde teenagers – a boy and a girl – both wearing madras shirts tucked into jeans. The boy, who lugged a black suitcase, looked like Brandon DeWilde from *Hud* except his jeans fit a little better. And the girl looked like Tuesday Weld with a slightly smaller nose.

They slumped on the couch.

"Five minutes," Doniphan said. "You're on."

"I'm Travis Mountjoy," the young man said. "This is my twin sister Mabel. We're astro-biologists."

Jeffries looked them over. "Cheryl?" he hollered at the ceiling.

"Yeah?" she called, down the hall.

"Sorry, kids," he said. "We got a heckuva lot of pitches today."

The receptionist peeked in. 'What is it?"

"Send the next pitch, *por favor*?"

"All the others left, Mr. Jeffries. Pretty quickly."

"Huh?"

"We sent them away," Travis said.

Jeffries yanked off his glasses. "You *what*?"

"When they heard our pitch, they left."

"Hmm. Must be a damn good pitch."

Mabel Mountjoy snapped her fingers. Two men in dark suits entered and applied handcuffs to the director. "Mr. Jeffries," she said. "By order of the U.S. Government, you are under arrest."

Travis assembled a video monitor on the conference table. "Enoch Jeffries," he opened a composition notepad, "you have violated ten counts of the U.S. Code Titles 16 and 18. Want to hear the charges?"

Jeffries said, wistfully, "Genius."

"You made a movie called *Unkillable* a few years ago," Travis said, aiming his remote at the monitor.

The screen flashed, showing three rats drifting in a fountain on the U.S. Capitol grounds. Soon, we discover, the rats are decoys attached to the scuba headgear of three female Navy SEALS with cascading, semi-curled hair. After toweling off, they storm the Capitol steps and make their way to a tall wooden door upon which they detonate a wad of explosive putty. A cobra-tattooed brunette leaps over the rubble and hoists a petrified senator by the necktie.

Travis hit pause. "There."

"What?" Jeffries said.

"Right there… behind her head."

"The nun-chucks?"

"The Great Seal of the United States Senate. Title 18 of the U.S. Code 713 – Use of likeness of the Great Seals of the U.S. House of Representatives or Senate…. Unauthorized use, manufacture--"

"Not bad," Jeffries said. "But not great, you know. You didn't live up to it."

"Let's keep going, Mr. Jeffries. You made another movie called *Jungles of Mars* about three years back."

"With pride."

"Great special effects, by the way. So, check this out…"

A spaceship wobbles in front of a red sky. Inside the cockpit, three pilots wrestle with the controls. Two of the men, in the throes of electrocution, implore the third to eject. He shoots out of the roof. A parachute deploys. As soon as he gains control he drifts, screaming, into a speeding flock of birds.

"Don't tell me," Jeffries said. "No birds on Mars?"

"No Yellow-Cheeked Warblers at any rate," Mabel said. "Ever

heard of the Migratory Bird Treaty?"

After some thought, Jeffries said, "C-minus."

"I don't think you understand the enormity of this, Mr. Jeffries. It's a federal crime. Title 16 USC 707. Any violation, knowing or unknowing, up to three years in prison...."

Doniphan raised his hand. "What about the, um, statute of limitations?"

Travis continued, "...not to mention transactions with countries supporting acts of international terrorism."

"What?"

"*Big Sheik on Campus*. Credits say 'Portions filmed in Libya'."

"A minor fabrication. We actually shot those scenes in Jackson Hole."

Travis dropped a folder at Jeffries' feet. "Ten counts. And per your question, Donnie, regarding the statute of limitations on the Migratory Bird Treaty... there *is* no statute of limitations on the Migratory Bird Treaty."

"Call me Doniphan, please."

"You know what this reminds me of?" Jeffries said. "*Séance on a Wet Afternoon*."

"Hit me," Doniphan said.

"Remember when the cops come for Kim Stanley and she, Richard Attenborough, and Gerald Sim gather 'round for one last séance, and in the middle of her trance *she can see* that they have already located the girl Richard abandoned in the woods and, for one moment, even though she's going to jail, everyone realizes she was a legitimate psychic after all?"

The room was silent.

"Nobody remembers?"

Mabel asked, "Is it black and white?"

"Yes."

"We're not allowed to watch old movies."

"Well," Jeffries said, "*that's* what I'm talking about."

Travis disassembled the video monitor. The sun cast a beam into the middle of the room, and everyone sat for a moment staring at the dust particles.

"So what do you think of our pitch, Mr. Jeffries?" Travis asked, shutting the briefcase.

Jeffries turned to Doniphan. "It started out a little iffy, huh?"

"I guess. Had some shock value, though."

"Then… Can't put my finger on it… but you kids had me. It was primal. I feared for my own well-being. Didn't you, Donnie?"

"I feared for yours, sir."

"It's honestly what I look for every Wednesday."

"I liked the intimidation factor," Doniphan said. "The Feds."

"Of course, the Feds." Jeffries rolled his eyes at the men on either side of him. "How tall are you, Kojak?" he asked. "Anyway, so, kids…. I guess what I'm saying is *I'm on board*, so to speak." He shrugged at Doniphan.

Travis and Mabel looked at each other and said, "Good."

Travis asked, "So what's the next step?"

"Well… I guess I should ask you that, yeah? I heard a great set-up, one that I will be *on board* for, as they say. Now I just need to know more about this… this movie."

"It's not a movie," Travis said. "It's a… situation."

"I see," Jeffries said. "If it's a *situation*… and, of course, not something involving attorneys and arraignment and all that jazz, then I guess we should figure out what we're going to shoot and when we're going to shoot it."

Mabel gestured to the cops, who un-cuffed Jeffries.

"What's the title?" Doniphan asked. "Out of curiosity."

"The name," Travis said, "is *Operation EMU*."

"Not so crazy about it."

"We start next month," Mabel said.

Jeffries shook out his wrists. "Can't do. We got pre-production for a Paramount project in three weeks."

"Push it back," Mabel said. "Or call your attorney."

Jeffries slipped off his visor and looked down at the carpet. Doniphan, across the room, whistled and stuck out his arm. Jeffries tossed the visor; it looped perfectly around Doniphan's finger and dropped to the floor.

"Sign this." Mabel held out a clipboard. "Security disclosure."

He signed.

"Congratulations, Mr. Jeffries. For the next six months, you're working for the U.S. Government. Everything you witness during this project is classified. Any disclosure, any recollections, any mention of this project in any way whatsoever to anyone – ever – and you will serve the maximum sentence per your felony violations in an offshore prison."

"Now *that* is genius," Jeffries said.

"You, too, Doniphan."

"Whatever," Doniphan said. "Mr. Jeffries, don't we need to ask them who they are maybe?"

"Good point, Donnie. You kids FBI or something?"

"NASA," Mabel said.

"Now." Travis flipped through his clipboard. "Take us to your Props department."

ii.

On a woodland reserve fifteen miles south of Virginia's Manassas National Battlefield, housed in a 6,000-square foot silo, is an enormous glass tank called the Natural Buoyancy Simulator. This tank holds 1.4 million gallons of pump-filtered, auto-chlorinated water, and is fitted with seventy-two observation portholes – 32 of which contain high-intensity lamps – and seven underwater cameras. Developed in the late 1960's, it still provides exemplary underwater simulation of zero-gravity conditions for NASA flight trainees.

Early one morning, three men in EVA space-flight suits stood on the catwalk surrounding the tank while a physical therapist tightened the laces on their red Converse All-Star sneakers, used to provide extra resistance in training. Meanwhile, a man in scuba gear sat on the edge and twirled a digital stopwatch.

"Ready when you are, gentlemen."

The man in the middle, Lt. Colonel Erasmus J.T. Clark, clamped the pressure tabs on his full-pressure, GEC Lexan helmet, took a running leap into the tank, and sunk slowly until he was just a blur.

"You can do it that way," the scuba instructor said, "or you can do laps first."

"Or tread water?" Captain T.W. Tongue yelled, his voice muffled by the helmet.

"Or tread water." The instructor inserted his mouthpiece and submerged.

Tongue jumped in and bobbed back to the surface, his arms sloshing like otters. "Coming in, Chief?" he yelled.

The last man standing, Colonel Nimrod T. Ashby, stared at his wobbly reflection. "Yes," he said. "I'm deciding on what to do first."

Ashby hated lying. He wasn't thinking about the exercises at all, but rather a letter he had written to his family the night before, which began:

Dear Marsha, Mandy, Jake, Felicity, Andrew, Jorge, Marcus and Rodge,
Seventeen days have passed since I left unexpectedly in the night and I wanted to let everyone know that I am doing fine.

Nothing gave him more pain than imagining Marsha and the kids reading the letter. Where would they read it? He pictured the kitchen table, or maybe the hearth in the den directly underneath the family photo taken after Rodge was born. Would Marsha read it aloud, or be too overcome? Would anyone cry? Would anyone think he was lying? The more scenarios, the more inadequate his letter had seemed for the purpose of delivering important information, as well as expressing sorrow.

I'm sure the family was alarmed when the white vans pulled up and the men came in with the pillowcase. You're never fully prepared for that kind of thing. From the day I transferred to the JFC Center in Houston, I assumed this or something similar would eventually happen. But, as

I said, you're never fully prepared. Incidentally, the men didn't hurt Daddy; they just wanted to make sure that no one – including myself -- knew where I was going. Does it make a little more sense now? I really hope so.

The instructor surfaced and Captain Tongue, who'd been hanging on the edge, quickly let go. The instructor glided under Ashby's high-tops. "You okay?"

Ashby watched his watery reflection break apart in ripples. "I am okay," he said. "I was thinking I might have left the Dynamic Escape Simulator running back at Goddard."

He really and truly hated lying. But sometimes the truth confused matters, especially the personal matters that no one else could understand or even cared about. Captain Tongue and Lt. Colonel Clark were single men; neither had children. They were young and had nothing to lose, nothing to live for but their day-to-day selves and their far-flung dreams.

I have some good news and some bad news. Daddy has been selected to go on a very important mission, and for security reasons I probably shouldn't say more. What I will say is that the research from this project will nullify many accepted theories about our existence in the universe, leveling the foundations of science, philosophy and religion. Your grandchildren will read about this mission in history books, though you will probably not. Which brings me to the bad news.

Ashby leaped into the tank – a fireman's leap, which created minimal splash and kept his head above water – and started the breaststroke toward the far edge, half the length of an Olympiccertified pool. The high-tops weighted his feet, so he tried scissor kicks to conserve energy and maximize flotation. He made his way to the far end and took a few breaths. He switched to freestyle on the return.

You will never see Daddy again. Therefore, I want to say a few words to everyone.

Ashby raised his arms and let his head submerge. Though it was dim underwater, he could see to the diving bell and airlock, where the instructor had locked Erasmus Clark in a bear hug, his fins kicking rapidly. Ahead, he could see Captain Tongue's shoelaces waving like jellyfish tentacles, and just beyond, large dark objects dropped into the water -- NASA-certified A/V viewfinders, soptometers and other dummy camera equipment – to be used later in a retrieval exercise.

Ashby reached the near edge. Moisture beads had spread across his EV Visor, making it harder to see. He looked above him just as the Panel Tech, in one go, switched on the tank's 38 high-intensity lights, illuminating the cylindrical ceiling and making the moisture look like so many stars.

Mandy, Jake, Felicity, Andrew, Jorge, Marcus and Rodge: I want everyone to behave. Do your chores, be honest, go to college and make a sincere effort to come home for Christmases. Mom may choose to get married again, which I completely understand. I want everyone to be accepting of this or any new situation. I only ask that you keep a picture of me displayed, and always think of me.

He suddenly felt tired. The horizontal strokes he'd used on

the way back had consumed too much energy, and he still had Treading Water and Equipment Retrieval phases, so he chose dogpaddle for the last lap. At a slow pace, he passed Captain Tongue, who raised his pressure glove for a high-five.

One more thing: you must be very careful what you say to people about Daddy going away -- friends, teachers, pastors and all trustworthy people included. A NASA counselor will visit in the next few weeks to help with the protocol of dealing with this matter of secrecy, and other things, like what this means exactly in terms of life insurance.

The scuba instructor burst through the surface with Erasmus Clark, whose helmet was filled with water and his thumbs up. Lab techs unclamped his helmet and pulled him onto the catwalk, where his suit emptied of water like a long-trolled fishnet.

Ashby waved at the instructor. "Beginning Tread Water phase."

"You're on the clock," the instructor said. He turned to Captain Tongue, who was clinging to the airlock buoy. "What about you, Chief?"

Tongue pushed off. "One more lap."

"He's really done two laps?" the instructor asked Ashby.

Ashby hunched and pushed on. He hated lying, even when it was merely an act of cold-hearted ambivalence.

•••

Later that night, on the grounds of the Goddard Flight Center in Maryland, Nimrod T. Ashby walked out of his wood-glowed bungalow to look at the stars, sizzling in the absence of a moon. For the last week he and his colleagues – Clark and Tongue – had been staying in NASA officers' quarters unused since the mid-sixties, replete with recliners, card tables, cork floors and wet bars: their last perk before the sedation physicals, transporter simulations and disorientation exercises; before they went under for good. He wandered barefoot across the half-acre of grass and waded into a small stream that cut through a meadow. On his last night of fresh air, he kept his same routine, doing what he'd always done in the evenings at home after all the kids were in bed and his wife had started her television show. Whenever he needed to calm himself, or be reminded of what made his soul feel alive, he looked up.

Now I want you all to remember one thing: Daddy is a man. As always, he is your father and, Marsha, your husband. He has raised you and supported you. He has loved you and considered your needs, feelings and dreams every day of his life. But remember that Daddy is a person with his own dreams. Ever since I was a little boy, I have wanted to go on a great journey, beyond all previous stakes and bounds, rising as high as a body can go. Now that I have this opportunity, I must take it or else I will feel like I haven't lived. I will always be your father, but I also want you to see me as somebody, great or small, who did something.
With love,
Daddy

iii.

On the west side of Reno, a brushed-chrome Greyhound Silverside rolled into the bus station and parked in Gate 14. The door hissed, the steps dropped, and one-by-one the passengers descended, wandering off through the depot. After the bus had emptied, the driver folded the funnies and checked his mirror: about eight rows back, he could see, dangling over an armrest, a pair of wrap-around wedge heels.

"Yo!" he called. He pulled himself out from the wheel and walked down the aisle, where he found, sprawled across the seats, a good-looking dirty blonde wearing corduroys with a macramé belt and a T-shirt that said, 'I'm Good: Just Ask Your Boyfriend." She had a cute face, long eyelashes and a button nose spotted with freckles, broad shoulders and a rack that rested on her chest like the ambrosia molds his mom used to make. He tapped her knee and noticed that her legs, sure enough, went all the way up to her ass.

"Holy smokes," she said, sitting up. "Nightmare." She slipped on a pair of magenta sunglasses and smiled. "Ever have one of those dreams where you're someplace familiar and part of you – the dreaming part – knows exactly where it is, but the waking part has no idea?"

"Baby, you are in Reno."

"Swell."

"And you are looking *good*," he said, easing in next to her.

She scooted over and yawned and looked out the window. A nun sitting on a blue Samsonite under a canopy waved and winked at her.

The driver, whom she noticed looked like a lecherous Jason Robards, put his hand on her knee and crept along her inseam until, on the verge of reaching her zipper, she reached in her purse and tucked a cold blade under his chin.

"What the hell is that?" he asked.

"A genuine stainless-steel Buck Knife."

"And this," said a deep voice above them, "is a double-barreled Phantom Series-E." A man in a black trench coat, standing in the aisle, held a gun to the driver's head.

The driver raised his hands and said, "Thank you for riding Greyhound," his keys jingling away down the aisle.

"Francine Dean?" the man asked, blowing the gun barrel.

"Yeah?"

"I'm your ride."

"Are you a cop?"

"I'm a second-unit director." Francine saw in his chalky face a sort of *Class*-era Andrew McCarthy, non-existent lips and all.

After rubbing a hand on his acid-wash jeans, he offered it to her. "I'm Doniphan Smith."

Francine used the Buck Knife to tuck a stray hair behind her ear. "And what about the Phantom gun thing?"

"It's a fake. Graphite." He handed it to her. "I carved it myself."

"You don't say."

"You can have it if you want."

"Swell."

●●●

Funny how things happen: Just a few weeks earlier, Francine – in a jade racer-back Tankini – lay on a large inner tube tied to a hovering helicopter, trying to look intense as the camera crew leaned in for a close-up. The other two contestants had lasted almost a minute in the air, which was going to be tough to beat. She grabbed hold of the straps as Mick Delfluvio came over with the mike.

"Francine, you gotta feel the pressure," he yelled.

"Yeah, Mick. I got my work cut out for me."

"What's your strategy?"

"Did a double knot on the straps here and just gonna not let go."

"Scared of falling?"

"Who isn't, Mick? But, you know, if I just adapt to the chopper surges and wind currents, I should be able to easily eclipse the one-minute mark."

"Try for the record?"

She smiled. "Do my best."

"Check!" he said, raising a thumb. "Ready?"

"Ready!"

The chopper surged fifty feet, hoisting the inner tube out over a man-made lake near a quarry. Immediately, Francine screamed and let go, flopping headfirst into the water.

A speedboat and two jet skis broke out from the docks, hurling life preservers and orange flotation devices. Divers pulled Francine aboard, where she was wrapped with towels and surrounded by a smaller camera crew. When she got to shore, the first unit crew had already continued to the mudslide toboggan event, leaving a small production team to prepare her for the exit interview and consolation-prize selection. They handed her a Dasani and an Indonesian-pattern sarong. As she approached the studio SUV, a man with a headset waved her in the direction of a pup-tent near a row of young evergreens. Inside she found, seated in foldout chairs, a good-looking teenage boy and girl dressed in yellow extreme weather gear. Behind them stood a man in a suit and mirrored sunglasses.

"Hi, Francine," the girl said. "Have a seat."

"Hi, is this a press junket?"

The boy said, "Francine, this is my sister Mabel Mountjoy. I'm Travis Mountjoy. We're astro--"

"Hold it," Mabel said. "We're television executives."

"Wow," Francine said, tucking back her wet hair. "How can I help you fine people?"

"Well," Mabel said. "You can start by being under arrest."

The man in the suit flashed a badge. Francine looked back at the tent opening, but there was another man blocking the way.

"Alright," Francine said, after the cuffs were applied. "What's the deal?"

"Last August," Mabel said, "did you appear in *Celebrity Gladiator Trivia Challenge*?"

"Um, yeah. I won it. "

"And earlier in January, were you a contestant on *Hottie Scavengers: Barbados*?"

"Certainly was."

"Did you know that it's illegal to appear on more than one game show per calendar year?"

"Huh?"

"Section 18, Article 456 of the U.S. Code."

"Listen, I just fell a hundred feet from a flying flotation device and you kids want to arrest me for hunting coconut monkey sculptures for charity?"

Mabel glanced at her notebook. "Oh, and you haven't paid taxes since… let's see… actually never. Yes. You've never paid taxes."

"Shit."

"Now, look," Travis said. "We know this is a lot to take in. What we're offering now is an option to avoid all jail time by participating in a community service program that will utilize your talents."

"My pottery?"

"Your acting."

"My acting. Okay."

"You were really good in *Learning Curves*, by the way," Travis said.

"Yeah, well… You saw that? How old are you?"

"We think you've got a special something that works with our project."

"Um, so this community service thing is like a movie? After-school special?"

The twins looked at each other and said, in unison, "A movie."

"Can I see a script?"

"No," Travis said.

"What's it about, then?"

Travis motioned for the officers to leave. He said, "Astronauts land on a planet similar to Earth except that it's eight to ten-thousand years behind us developmentally."

"So, everyone's… *special?*"

"They are prehistoric men and women on the cusp of civilization."

"What happens?"

Travis and Mabel looked at each other again. Now that Francine had had a good look at him, the boy looked awfully similar to Leif Garrett in *The Outsiders*, and the girl like a young, blonde version of the woman who got stoned to death in *Zorba the Greek*.

"We'll *see* what happens," Travis said.

"I need a little more here, kids," Francine said. "Like, would you say it's a cross between *Clan of the Cave Bear* and, maybe, *Total Recall*?"

"I don't understand what you're saying," Mabel said.

"Okay. Like, *Runaway Bride* is a cross between *Pretty Woman* and *My Best Friend's Wedding*. See?"

Mabel thought for a moment.

"Well, not *Total Recall*," Travis said. "That's set on a colonized alien planet in the future. We're talking about something back in time."

"But actually in the future," Mabel said.

"Okay, alright." Francine sighed. "Work with me, kids."

"*Clan of the Cave Bear* fits. Cross that with *The Right Stuff*?"

"Sounds a little long. *Apollo 13*?"

"Make it *Space Cowboys*," Travis said. "And we got a deal."

"Can I bring my Portuguese Water Dog?"

"No."

"And what's the benefit to me again?"

"You won't go to jail and you won't have to pay $150,000 in back taxes."

"Whew. Time flies."

"Now," Mabel said. "Before you sign the security clearance forms, we need to ask you to do one kind of semi-crucial thing to see if you're right for the part."

"What's that?"

"Squat," Travis said.

Francine hesitated.

"It's okay with the handcuffs and everything. Just squat real quick with your feet flat on the ground... without your heels rising."

Francine stood up. "It seems kind of gross."

"You'd be surprised," Travis said. "Not everyone can do it."

"And why would I be doing this again?"

Mabel pointed at the ground. "Squat... Feet... Flat."

Francine, looking aside, lowered into a squat.

They never aired Francine's inner-tube debacle on the season finale of *Death Perception*, nor did she get the chance to choose from the consolation prize tent; but two months later, after finding a place for her dog and breaking up with a boyfriend who hadn't called her in a month, she found herself riding in a Jeep with a guy named Doniphan and a fake Phantom Series-E pistol with a spring-lock chamber in her lap.

Once they'd merged onto Interstate 80, an hour south of Reno, he tossed Francine a manila folder.

"Your dossier."

Francine opened the folder.

Welcome, Francine
Upon entry into the Stribling Valley Campsite you will be known as:
Name: Luhk
Age: 5,085 (Solar Revs)
Profession: Weaver of baskets, spouse
Male Possessor: Beyzore (Huntsman)
Children: None (barren)

Character Profile:
You are skittish, hunched, yet postured. A servitudinal life punctuated
by beatings and humiliations has made you sullen. You never smile.
You have a nervous tick you do sometimes, flaring your nostrils,
holding your index finger up and flicking it like shooing flies. This is
the result of your many, many years in servitude, not to mention the
beatings and humiliations. You are attractive. Your bust is big and
sometimes you stick it out when stretching, after carrying water from
the creek for instance. You are ridiculously loyal. You are devoted to
your Male Possessor (Beyzore) because he protects you from other
male possessors and gives you a sense of belonging. You are barren.
Your inability to have children has made you ashamed and guiltfully
attached to your male possessor. You have had numerous conflicts with
your Male Possessor over this issue. Males in this tribe tend to believe
that the woman is the object of blame in matters of reproductivity
and sexual dysfunction, but a sliver of doubt has entered his mind
over the years and he suspects that you lust other male possessors and
covet their livestock. Character keywords: subservient, smoldering,
stretching, dependent, postured, busty, forgetful, nervous.

Character Costume:
While you are a valued tribal member due to your weavings,
attractiveness and/or helpfulness, you are not affluent and therefore
you wear a garment commensurate with your status in society.

1.   Wooden earrings (see Makeup)
2.   Bearskin* waist cloth
3.   Blue Paint** (see Props)

*The bearskin should be fully tanned and dried before you receive it.
 Please inform Wardrobe if you detect an odor.
**Props will discretely apply the Blue Paint. The purpose of the blue
 paint is ornamental, slathered on the torso of all concubines under
 age 8,000 (Solar Revs). The Blue Paint is not open to debate, creative
 or political. It is a lead-free base.

"That's your Character Card."

Francine leafed through the security forms, a two-page employment contract and various diagrams of hunched, prehistoric people who were really difficult to look at. "It's a lot to take in," she said. "So this is a caveman kind of thing?"

"Mr. Jeffries will explain everything."

"Oh, fuck. Enoch Jeffries is directing?"

Doniphan pulled onto a gravel road that cut through a row of foothills, bare except for patches of cagey, quivering tumbleweed.

"Problem?"

"He's just a prick." She aimed the pistol out the window. "He asked me to take my shirt off when I auditioned for *Hail Mary* a few months ago."

"Some of his toughest decisions come down to that, Francine."

She turned the pistol over to see the letters

DONIPHAN S

carved under the barrel. "I was like, 'this is for the part of the neurosurgeon,' and besides, I did not want to kow-tow to that perverted little midget."

"Kow-tow?" He held out a pack of cloves.

Francine took one. "Do you have any idea how it feels to have a room full of people critique your naked body?"

"Sorry if this sounds forward, but you've, um, done more topless than Johnny Weissmuller."

"Well…" Francine said. "I'm thirty now."

They passed over the foothills and came upon a broad, sun-blasted desert, the flatness surging here and there with flat-topped mesas just like the ones in *Close Encounters* and *Poltergeist 2*.

Francine unwrapped the yellow ribbons of her wedge heels

and propped her bare feet on the dashboard. "Doniphan, let me be straight with you: I've been working in movies since I was eighteen." She pressed the car lighter. "They may not have been big movies and I may not have been anything but third-string…" The lighter popped. "But here's the deal: I'm thirty now, and it's painfully obvious that, whatever kind of career I've gotten myself by now, I'm realizing that my breasts are not going to take me to the next level."

"I can't *wait* to see you slathered in blue paint."

She tossed the clove out the window. "I can't smoke that." She touched her big toe, polished like a caramel apple, and noticed, in front of the car, a pair of jackrabbits scatter from one dry bush to another. "You know, last night I watched myself in *Beach Wedding*, and I couldn't stand it, my body. The scene where I'm changing out of my nurse's uniform at the dialysis center…. I sat there thinking, that's all I have, you know, and it's served up to the whole world."

"Come on," Doniphan said. "You look absolutely fantastic."

"It's not about looks, Doniphan. It's about mystique. I want mine back again."

Three hours later, in the middle of nowhere, they came upon a white canopy sheltering two young women with bellybutton rings and walkie-talkies the size of baguettes.

Doniphan lowered his window. "Francine Dean arriving."

One of the girls flipped papers on a clipboard. "Dean… Dean… D… D… Francine! *Talent*." She hoisted her walkie-talkie. "This is Breaker One. Sending Talent through. Read?"

Affirmative.

They drove through a barbwire Army check-post and had their undercarriage sniffed by German shepherds, continued past a row of hangars and up a muddy incline. At the crest

Francine looked out upon a scene of broad arid desolation, the Earth cracked by meandering crevices, clawed by tumbleweed, the entire scene pitilessly beaten by the sun.

"Welcome to Shacklett Air Force Base," Doniphan said.

The windows lowered, the moon-roof slid open and she felt gusts of dry air.

"Ready?" Doniphan asked.

"Sure."

He slammed on the accelerator. She grabbed the armrests. The Jeep swerved down the incline, but picked up a terrific speed headlong across the desert. Francine thought she heard, above the wisps of wind, a sound like a lawn mower, growing so intense she could feel it sucking at her chest, reaching a piercing level as a broad B-1 Bomber coasted across their path.

"Faaaaak!" Doniphan screamed, as the Jeep spun sideways and the brakes screeched before coming to a halt.

Francine lowered her sunglasses and looked down the side of the Jeep at the mile-wide crater that had almost swallowed them. "What in the hell is that?"

"The Stribling Valley."

She looked over the edge. The cliff-side grooves meandered around ledges and hanging rocks and strange black streaks to a gray ground that had the look of a dirty sub-layer of beach sand. From that view it seemed large enough to contain a small town.

Doniphan continued, "It's actually a meteor crater, not a natural valley. It was formed 30,000 years ago by a 75-foot, mushroom-shaped lump of iron from space."

"No, Doniphan, what is *that*?" she said, pointing.

"The tail broke entering our atmosphere and lagged behind the main meteor's impact, which was huge – equivalent to a 5-megaton nuclear blast – and the tail settled on a wave of rolling firmament and became the big rock structure over there in the corner: The Jarlsburg Butte, so named by famished Dutch explorers in 1675."

"Okay, enough. What is *that*?" Francine pointed at a small group of people surrounding what looked like a twenty-foot polar bear with a woman hanging on its neck.

Doniphan leaned over her. "Oh, that's an *Eremotherum*, a prehistoric giant three-toed sloth."

The hanging woman, wearing Army fatigues, barked orders at a guy fiddling with a large antenna. She eventually slid down and seized the antenna and soon the creature was raising its arms and stepping forward. The group cheered, high-fived and wandered off behind a camouflage tarp.

"Props." Doniphan said. "Love those fuckers."

And the man called Meemaw, son of Quapaw, Cherokee and Comanche, also known as Warm Blood, son of Hot Blood of the Moonlight Battles Where the White Wolf Descended From the Three Weeping Stars and during which many souls were sent to the Lazy River of Oblivion; this man, the one they called Meemaw, accepted the rug of the chieftain, as bequeathed to him by the people -- his father's people -- and they sat down to savor the mulled entrails of a white bull.

--<u>Aboriginal America: An Oral History</u>, Marlana P. DeSoto, trans., ed., 1995

iv.

Dr. Emil Dunn, the resident psychiatrist at Goddard Flight Center, got the emergency page around noon. Earlier that morning an astronaut-in-training had gone stiff in the Anti-Gravity Simulator. His symptoms had remained unchanged after several hours.

"So, why can't he move exactly?" Dunn asked the general practitioner, Felicia Lang. They stood over the patient, his arms in a frozen embrace like a dead raccoon.

"Not quite sure, Emil," Dr. Lang said. "Hoping you could help."

Dunn checked the astronaut's pulse and asked for the chart.

"Lt. Colonel Erasmus J.T. Clark," he read. "Where did he come from, again?"

"Zero-Gravity. The duty tech said he was inside four days."

Dunn lifted Clark's eyelids and shined a penlight.

"Maybe some kind of Carpal Tunnel attack?"

"Could be." Dunn pinched Clark's thumb and tried to move his arm. "Or Post Traumatic Stress. Any B.P.D. on record?"

Dr. Lang flipped through the clipboard. "Doesn't say. He's a highly decorated Air Force Colonel. Light combat in the Gulf, climbed the ranks at D.O.D. Cherry-picked by NASA six weeks ago for something."

"I think I know what this might be. Who brought him in?"

The door slammed shut, and two teenagers wearing matching white overalls stood before them.

"Dr. Dunn," Lang said. "Drs. Travis and Mabel Mountjoy. They work for CHETO."

"And that is…?"

"Clandestine Human/Extra-Terrestrial Operations."

"Ah." Dunn shook their hands. "So, do we know what he was doing in the A.G.S. when he… um… got like this?"

"We do," Mabel said, offering a bag of Corn Nuts around. "He was using the roll-on cuff to apply the urinary relief tube to his penis."

"Ah ha," Dunn said, glancing at Dr. Lang, who looked away.

"That's the urine collection apparatus," Travis said.

"Understood," Dunn said. "Have you observed any abnormal behavior during his training?"

Travis went to the wall, put his palms flat against it and spread his legs, like he was about to be frisked. "You mentioned earlier that you had an idea what was wrong."

Dunn peeled off his glasses. "Solipsism Syndrome."

For a moment, they contemplated this.

"Isn't Solipsism a widely refuted theory?" Mabel asked.

"As a philosophical concept, yes. As a psychological concept, it's gaining ground, especially in orbiting astronauts."

"Spell it out for me, Doctor," Travis said, turning around. "Because I am in serious doubt, and I actually don't know what that means."

"Solipsism is the belief that the only reality is one's own reality, that anything beyond individual experience is non-existent. Astronauts who endure weeks of weightlessness, delayed communication, claustrophobia and diminished stimulation have the tendency to lose their sense of reality, so to speak, and react to the hostile and cold surroundings of space by conceiving that all external substance is just a product of the imagination."

"But doesn't the astronaut observe his fellow astronauts' reactions to stimuli – for example, the taste of thermo-stabilized beef – and realize that there's a social context to reality?"

"In this state, it wouldn't even register." Dunn approached the examining table. "Dr. Mountjoy, look at this man." He ran a reflex implement under the astronaut's foot. "He's catatonically withdrawn."

"Check it out," Travis said. "He looks like one of those blow-up sex dolls."

Mabel guffawed, and elbowed her brother. "Dr. Dunn," she said, "it's very, very important that we continue his training *soon*."

"Is he going to MIR?"

Travis scratched his ear.

"Has he been quarantined long?"

Mabel chomped some Corn Nuts.

"Look," Dunn said. "I'm going to recommend a massive dose of Valium."

"Okay." Mabel patted the doctor's arm. "Call us when he thaws out."

The moment the door shut Erasmus Clark's arms dropped, his body relaxed and he began to breathe deeply.

Dr. Lang wrapped his arm with a blood pressure strap.

"Where am I?"

Dunn checked the pressures. "Colonel Clark, I'm Dr. Dunn, this is Dr. Lang. You're in the infirmary here at Goddard. What's the last thing you remember?"

"Whoa." Clark rubbed his eyes. "Let's see... I think I was floating in front of the waste management compartment in Anti-Gravity."

"And what happened?"

"The applicator cuff was too big for my… you know… thing. My urine was, uh, floating all around me and that's the last thing I remember."

Dunn grabbed a chair. "Colonel Clark, I want to ask you a few questions. How long have you been quarantined here?"

"Four weeks. Five? Don't know. We just started Time Disorientation."

"Are you training for a particular mission?"

"Yes."

"May I ask what it is?"

"It's a… particular mission."

"I see. Have you had any contact with your family?"

"No family."

"Girlfriend?"

"No… contact."

"Colonel, I'm going to leave you, but I want you to be very careful during your training and subsequent… mission. I suspect you may suffer from a Borderline Personality Disorder that triggers a debilitating muscular stress. It's the only way I can explain this stiffness you suffered today."

"I feel better, Doc."

"You don't want to freeze-up like that on a mission."

"I feel better."

Left alone in the examining room, Erasmus Clark stared at the ceiling. He listened to his breathing, his heartbeat, his digestion, hoping to hear something. He wondered if he'd injured himself during training and not realized it, or maybe ignored some stress issue that had now manifested itself as an affliction. But, of course, he was fooling himself: He knew exactly what was wrong.

From an early age, Clark had learned how to avoid problems. He avoided his father, a smug, self-important bank manager, and his stepmother, a detached woman who always wore bathing suits around the house, by withdrawing to his room to read about great adventurers and to day-dream about becoming one of his *Star Wars* figures, abandoning his inanimate household by slipping forever inside the guts of his *Open-Belly Tauntaun* toy.

Since then, he'd grown up and made a life for himself in the armed services; yet, he was learning that while his avoidance of problems had protected him to some extent, it had also cocooned him in immaturity. Relationships came and went, usually women who didn't mind him traveling around the country for test-flight projects. Eventually they tired of this, and of his need, even after being away, to have his own space, and to fulfill arbitrary career goals that pushed him up the officer ranks in the direction of... *where?* For a time, he considered the military a perfect career fit; he could start a family and settle in Washington and maybe one day reach the level of single-star General. He'd already bought a house in Arlington and joined an officer's country club, where he golfed and ate in the grill several times a month to fulfill the membership quota. He eventually got a transfer out of the Air Force to serve as a congressional liaison on military appropriations. And it was around this time that he met Adele Deet, a policy review attorney for the Senate Armed Services Committee.

Clark and his friend John Sykes were talking into their drinks at a fundraiser when Adele appeared out of nowhere.

"I'm not going to eat these after all," she said, holding out a plate of nut-coated cheeseballs. She had short brown hair and a confident demeanor -- the kind of person you could fall into and disappear forever.

For their first date, they went to a lobster place across the river in Alexandria. They talked nervously and he left a 45% tip. After dinner, they walked along the docks among the people who had escaped from their houses, while overhead the stars dimmed behind a cloudy haze with a strong half moon burning through. They strolled and talked about living on boats and Shaker furniture and going back in time. At the end of the evening, he took her home to Foggy Bottom and they hugged awkwardly in front of her doorman.

The next day they were fucking. It began with them talking outside the Hart Senate Office Building, and it was well after six, so Clark asked if she wanted a ride home. While they drove down Constitution on a string of green lights, Adele stuck her hand in his pants and squeezed him until he could barely breathe. The next thing he knew, his pants were down and she was leaning over the emergency break and he had no idea what city he was in anymore. Rumbling across the George Washington Bridge in third gear, he came like his very life had been torn out and was wriggling on a hook.

As the weeks went on he grew more obsessed with everything they'd done and talked about. Nights alone his body ached, as if her blood ran through him, and he had strange dreams about climbing a set of stairs that started at her feet, reaching the wide, clear crow's nest of what she saw with her eyes and how her nose itched when it was raining outside and she was alone.

Another month went by and their passion settled. Instead of just making love and sleeping, they started going out in public again, to dinner, to movies, sometimes parties. But now there was an understanding that they were a couple, clinging to each other as if the world wanted to break them apart.

He began to grow intensely jealous. If he came upon her

in the halls of the Capitol talking to a man, he became flushed, almost speechless, and often he would walk away without saying anything, telling himself that, no matter what, he would somehow be abandoned.

It didn't help matters that, around this time, Adele asked Clark if they could have a threesome with his best friend, John Sykes.

He sat there in silence, feeling like he was going to fall through the chair. Adele responded by breaking into tears, offering trite explanations for why she was so desperate to feel loved, objectified and worshipped with such a passionate desire that the feeling would explode with the most intense aftershocks. She rambled. She stood up and sat down and paced in front of him, as if she were in a lecture hall. Then she sat down in the most unattractive slump with her leg over the arm of the chair, and assumed the demeanor of someone who was making a one-time offer. She was determined to continue this self-discovery by trying everything possible, which included being with two men at once, and hoped in her heart it could be transformed into something loving and carefree, spiritual, and shared with someone she loved from the very bottom of her heart, like Clark, rather than with a stranger.

Without a word Clark went back to his house in Arlington. He took a long shower, watched a classic Duke-North Carolina game on ESPN and thought about all the things Adele had said about growing up the ugly duckling, and how it had led her to chalk unsettled scores with people in her adult life whose only crime was that they reminded her of those who had not loved her.

He rolled over on the couch and let the pain spread until he fell into a tense sleep. He woke in the middle of the night and tried to call her, but she didn't answer and he didn't leave a message. The next morning, he called in sick. When he came back to work the following day, miraculously, the people from NASA were there with the offer to move on to something new. He accepted without even hearing the details.

And now, in the Goddard infirmary examination room, staring up at the asbestos tiles in the ceiling, he wondered where he fit among Adele's unsettled scores, tucked deep inside her dollhouse, stuffed into the wrong clothes, affixed to the wrong chair, staring blankly out a window.

V.

Standing under the Jarlsburg Butte -- a round, three-story rock cradled in a base like an egg -- Francine had the unsettling feeling that at any moment it could hatch.

Doniphan, standing on the far side of the rock, waved for her to follow. Under the boulder an iron stairwell descended, curving around a cement column. The passageway, glowing with small blue light fixtures, led down to a steel door. Doniphan turned the handle and they entered a room that looked similar to a bygone dentist's reception area, with a broad wooden desk, a rotary telephone, upholstered chairs and a glass table with built-in ashtrays. The entire back wall was mirrored except for a door on the far right.

Doniphan led her into a lounge area with La-Z-Boy recliners, split level coffee tables and an L-shaped couch. Several healthy looking people in sweats were watching *The Prisoner* on the wood-paneled television.

Doniphan whistled. "Hey, this is Francine Dean." Nobody budged.

Past the lounge was a dormitory, the rooms mostly bare with bunk beds tucked with rough green blankets and flat pillows, unpacked duffels, make-up organizers, music players, packs of smokes and strewn clothes. In some rooms, people were unpacking, fooling with unreceptive cell phones, stretching languidly or traipsing about in a state of self-conscious nakedness; actors, every one of them. Doniphan led Francine to a room with a small wooden table and a hanging hooded light.

"What the hell is this place?" She tossed her bag on the top bunk.

"The Cave."

Francine shrugged.

"Want to see something cool down the hall?"

Doniphan took her to a pitch-black room. After he switched on the light, Francine looked upon a large wood-paneled wing surrounded on all sides by pea-green curtains, with three-dimensional glass maps, video panels, circuit boards, ditto machines, a globe stuck with red pins, rotary-dial phones, a recording console with tape reels hanging off the spools, a glass gun case with EMERGENCY in red letters and – taking up the entire far corner – a gigantic mainframe computer.

"Is this where they filmed *Hunt for Red October*?"

Doniphan picked up a red telephone. "Deploy the long-range warheads, General!" he said, in a Jimmy Stewart voice.

"Don't!" Francine yelled.

"It's okay, it's dead. The line's dead."

"I'm kidding, dip-shit. So, what's the story?"

"Used to be some kind of secret command center, I'm told." Quoting with his fingers, he continued, "the *people who back us* set us up here for the *accommodations*. It's nothing now, just part of the *Air Force base* we're in right now."

"Stop doing that." Francine tapped a keyboard. "Looks like one of those places they kept aliens."

"No comment."

"I'm not staying here," she said. "No way in hell."

"It's okay." He showed her the door. "This is just a Cold War leftover. It's nothing. They built and tested some aircraft out here is all."

When they got back to Francine's room, they found a woman in a HOOTERS outfit weeping on the bottom bunk.

"Francine, Gail," Doniphan said. "I'll fetch you guys for Orientation in ten."

Francine sat next to her. "Wanna talk?" she asked the weeping woman, a petite gal with a face that was pretty, but innocent and dull; and a dead-ringer for the thin blonde chick who left after the first season of *Facts of Life*.

She offered her a Certs.

"Thanks. I'm okay. Just a little homesick."

"Yeah, it sucks here."

"I – I just got yelled at," she said.

"Who yelled at you?"

"Out there in the lounge..."

Francine got up. In the hallway – waiting for her, it seemed – was a shorthaired woman in rolled-up cammo pants, jackboots and a green t-shirt with a pack of smokes rolled in the sleeve, holding a wooden spear: a young Billy Jean King crossed with a thin Rosie O'Donnell.

"You want a piece of this?" the woman asked, raising her spear. Francine recognized her as the woman who was riding the giant sloth when she arrived.

"You want a piece of *this*?" Francine replied, showing her middle finger.

"You'll get your props soon," she said, stomping away.

When Francine returned to the room, Gail was changing. She had a nice little aerobic instructor's body, with a retro tan line like the kid in the old Coppertone ad.

"What's with the HOOTERS gear?"

] 39 [

"I concierge at the Vegas hotel." She slipped on a white tennis skirt and a striped plunge-neck halter-top.

"Oh, I see," Francine said. "HOOTERS Hotel?"

"Yeah. It's okay. Mainly golfers."

"What movies have you done?"

"No movies."

"You're not an actor?"

"Nope."

"Hmm. That's weird. Mind if I peek at your Character Card?"

"I've done some magazines. A couple of spreads."

"Oh, shit!" Francine said, slapping her forehead.

"What?"

"Shit!"

Gail covered her mouth. "What?"

"That troll out there with the stick…. She's Props. Fuck! *She's* the one who's going to be applying blue paint to our tits."

"Is that bad?"

"That is a big-time travesty."

Many agrarian tribes of this period [1690-1790] were self-sufficient and not inclined to trade, especially with Europeans. The reasons were twofold. Tribal mentality bred a distrust of foreigners and, second, self-sufficiency was a matter of deeply felt pride. Once the English, French, Spanish and Scandinavian settlers had established themselves in various outposts, the trading of handmade goods, maize and other products for guns, alcohol and tobacco became commonplace and led to what modern historians view as a major catalyst for the damage of Native American productivity and psyche.... The one tribe that proved an exception, based on its oligarchic, visionary and some might say paranoid leadership, was the Nevada Meemaw, who resisted the European trade overtures with some of the most violent and senseless retaliations on record.

--G. Phillip Wells, <u>Tribes of Destiny</u>, 1977

vi.

Captain Tongue lay on a bed in the Goddard Flight Center dormitory, staring at the ceiling, his cheeks puffed like balloons. Before he could exhale, the door knocked and opened.

"T.W.?" a lab tech said. "Gimbal Rig in five."

His cheeks still puffed, hands behind his head, Tongue nodded.

"Need a moment?"

Tongue nodded.

"I'll be back in two."

Tongue held up two fingers and nodded.

"By the way, your clock's wrong. It's actually 11:26am." The lab tech slammed the door.

Tongue exhaled a gust of smoke, flicked away the joint and soaked his thumb in a glass of bedside Tang. "Fucking time disorientation." He swatted the hovering cloud until it broke apart like a yolk, then he got on the floor and found the roach, which he swallowed.

"Wow." He beat his chest. "This is gonna hurt."

He went to the small square mirror by the door, patted the bristles of his peppery crew cut and checked his eyes for redness. He picked up his morning schedule card.

Captain T.W. Tongue
6:00am – Cardio-Fitness and Endorphin Measurements (South Field)
7:15am – Continental Breakfast (Officers' Mess)
8:00am – Mass-Driver Asteroid Tug Troubleshooting (Blue A/V Room)
9:00am – Intergalactic Waste Management (Magenta Conference Room)
10:00am – Moon Rover Relays (Recreation Field West)
10:30am – Break

11:30am -- MASTIF (Gimbal Rig) Training

He planted his foot on the floor and concentrated on his balance, his breathing, his fluctuating high, waiting with an ever-mounting sense of dread for the lab guy to return.

As hard as he tried to let his mind go blank, he couldn't avoid the painful memories of January's Super Bowl: the Pop Warner Jr. Pee-Wee Division II Super Bowl, held every year at Disney's Wide World of Sports complex in Lake Buena Vista, Florida.

On a crisp, breezy day it was south versus north as the NASA-sponsored Dripping Springs, Texas, Green Martians squared off against the Syracuse, New York, Mighty Lumberjacks – two of the most efficient Jr. Pee-Wee 8-9-10-year-old squads in recent memory. With three minutes to go in the game, the Green Martians led 6-0 after a hard-fought touchdown with a failed conversion attempt. The Martians' excellent defensive squad held off a Mighty Lumberjacks' comeback with an interception at the Martian's 30-yard line, returned to midfield by free safety Mitch O'Dell. And now the pride of Dripping Springs was gainfully running the ball, working the clock and letting thoughts stray to that four-tiered trophy and the Li'l Champs Gift Packs from Hershey's.

Lest anyone forget, Coach T.W. Tongue had *warned* the squad about Mighty Lumberjacks outside linebacker Gregg Fonseca – Pop Warner Football's largest player – who had terrorized Upstate New York squads with his uncanny athleticism, blazing speed and unapologetic demeanor. Coach Tongue had *shown* them film and photos, had *drawn* diagrams of his blitzing techniques, even *quizzed* them on the double-team schemes he'd designed to stop the kid. *Never count him out!*

Tongue swore the kid had to be older than nine. In the days leading up to the big game, he asked a few friends in the security profession to find out if this 110-pound, five-and-a-half foot tall yahoo was really and truly a Pee-Wee. When everything came up clean, he approached the league rep about the weight issue, arguing for emergency weight limits to balance the playing field against Fonseca; but the rep begged off any weight restrictions, as some parents had created a gallstone epidemic by putting their kids on high protein diets.

In truth, it wasn't the size and weight of Gregg Fonseca that really irked Captain Tongue. It was his *mullet*. Dangling out the back of his football helmet hung the longest, straightest, gnarliest rat-tail he'd ever seen – almost to the kid's waist – and it made him sick just thinking about it. Not merely a fashion statement, this hairdo served as a kind of plumage of his football dominance. A fellow Pop Warner coach from Albany sent Tongue a scouting video in which this oversized lummox leaped over the entire line, his mullet flying behind him like a May Day streamer as he pulverized the other team's quarterback.

And now, with the clock winding down, Tongue expected desperate measures from Fonseca and the Mighty Lumberjacks. The Green Martians tackles were creating amazing holes for running back Cedric Midgely, while on the other side of the ball, the 'Jacks blitz packages had little effect. And, much to Coach Tongue's satisfaction, the Martian tight ends' intense double-teams had neutralized Fonseca's furious rushes up the middle.

With a minute thirty-four in regulation, the Mighty Lumberjacks burned a timeout – their second. Tongue called his squad to the sidelines and instructed Alan Stivell, his quarterback, to milk the clock, stay in the pocket and trust his blockers. The whistle blew and the squads took the field. On second down and seven, the Green Martians ran the ball – gaining just two yards. Alan, from the huddle, looked to the sidelines for the next play. Tongue contemplated a pass, but thought it foolish to risk the interception; then again, if the Green Martians didn't gain five on the next play they'd be punting and giving the 'Jacks a chance, however small, to take the game. Tongue's gut said, *believe in the ground game.* Ultimately, this was a chess match, and he chose the safe move: to fake the run by appearing to go with the pass but sticking with the run anyway. He signaled a *fake sweep option.* Alan took it to the huddle and they broke.

Watching his team line up in stance, Tongue got that warm feeling, like water settling into sand, a realization that all the unwieldy forces of life had been checked, the only thing left being his own will; which made it all the more painful that he let his focus wander to the defensive backfield, zeroing in on Gregg Fonseca. Because what he saw at that moment made his jaw drop. Not only was this narrow shouldered, fat-gutted swine child *looking at him* in what was without question a provoking way, but doing so with his super-size mullet draped over his shoulder, *stroking it* like a pet ferret.

Tongue called for a play change. Alan looked confused, but told Cedric the new play and signaled to the receivers. This play – the turning point of the game – would be a *flea-flicker*: a hand-off to the running back, who pitches it back to the quarterback, who throws it to the designated receiver. However, this play did not call for the five yards needed for a first down, but for as far as the kid could throw – fifteen yards – into the hands of the right flanker and, by God, Pop Warner history. And it had to be done this way. Tongue wouldn't settle for that kind of cocksure provocation, especially from a nine-year-old anomaly.

Alan did a hard count. The defense didn't flinch. He hiked the ball and handed it to Cedric, who pitched it back. Meanwhile, the tight ends and fullback – three strong pups – zeroed in on Fonseca. But a defensive tackle burst through the line, pummeling Alan and knocking the ball loose.

Tongue had no reason to panic just yet. Yes, the ball was loose – never a good thing – but his quarterback was about to fall on it. Even if a Mighty Lumberjack *somehow* took possession, he would have a hell of a forty-yard run back in the opposite direction if he wanted to score. Sure enough, Alan retained possession. But instead of falling on the ball and taking the sack, he tried to run. Suddenly, parting the entangled bodies like a Wendigo through the tundra, Fonseca stripped the ball out of Alan's hands and scooped it up. Cedric tried to make the tackle, as did several linemen, but they all dashed upon an impenetrable stiff-arm. Tongue watched, dumbfounded, as the rat-tail waved to him ceremoniously in the direction of the end zone and, for all intents and purposes, the game.

A change befell Captain Tongue: The established lines between coach, player and fan blurred. As if from outside of his body, he saw his clipboard drop and a lightning bolt flash in front of him. The rest went blank.

Looking back, it didn't surprise him one bit – his reaction. He'd spent so long in preparation, thinking like his opponent, seeing like his quarterback, feeling anguish like the parents and fans, that he didn't really realize – until he actually had his hands around the mullet and was dragging Gregg Fonseca to the ground ten yards from the end zone – that he had in fact crossed an established line.

Hours later, leaning against the Chuck E. Cheese Bandstand with an ice pack on his eye while the kids cried over their pizza, he berated each and every one of them for letting the moment slip from their grasps. But by the time he got around to making a point of blaming himself, he kn ew he'd lost them.

•••

The MASTIF (Multiple Axis Space Test Inertia Facility), also known as the Gimbal Rig, tested an astronaut's ability to control a wayward spacecraft, requiring him to stabilize three spinning aluminum cages while spinning within the vortex.

Captain Tongue sat in a padded chair affixed to the large metal axis.

"Any questions, Captain?" the lab tech called up.

"Yeah, I guess my question is why am I doing this?" He wished he hadn't eaten that roach.

"To simulate and resolve complex tumbling motions that might occur in orbit."

"No duh. What I'm asking is… if I'm being sedated for the Launch and Encounter situations in a remotely controlled transporter, what is the point of me spinning around in this for three hours?"

"Five hours, actually."

"Fucking hell."

"At the very least it will test your physiological tolerance, eye oscillation and capacity for motion sickness."

"My capacity for that will be especially large today."

The nitrogen jets ignited with a piercing hiss.

"Let me know when you're ready to tumble," the lab tech yelled, affixing his headset.

The cages now spun around him while the whole contraption hummed.

"I'm saying," Tongue said into the headset receiver, "I'm probably going to vomit."

"That's okay. I'll keep everything documented." The lab tech violently tapped on the console keyboard. "I'll get the roll, pitch and yaw cages moving in combo. Then we'll try some three-way tumbling."

"Surely people have puked in here before."

"Maybe."

"It must go everywhere," Tongue said, his voice droning in his ears, swallowed by the glaze of slowness forming around him. He tried to interpret the motions on the monitor, but his eyes weren't capturing the specifics of sight, just the generalizations.

The lab tech's voice, through the headphones, sounded a million miles away. *I'll control it until the three-way tumbling, then I'll switch to Pilot and you're on.*

Tongue stared into the green monitor a foot away from his nose, almost to the point of seeing through it, or spinning inside it, until the looping cages blurred into nebulous and suggestive shapes. He seized the joysticks.

About to switch to Pilot.

The jets kicked full blast while the cages whirled ferociously in tandem.

Switching to Pilot, Captain Tongue.

Tongue wobbled the joysticks. His stomach boiled.

You're on, Captain! Attempt synchronization!

"Here goes!" Tongue yelled, and a tremendous belch echoed through the rotunda.

The lab tech immediately ducked under a commemorative Hubble Telescope Launch poncho.

vii.

Francine, lying on the top bunk in a pink tube top and zipper pocket jeans, was flipping through a *Vogue* when Doniphan knocked.

"Kick-off meeting, hot stuff."

After peeking in a compact, she climbed down, slipped on some cork heels and followed the other stragglers to a conference room with fluorescent lights and a long granite table with white plastic containers all around. Francine found her box and sat down, recognizing some faces from the audition circuit.

Then she caught sight of Enoch Jeffries caressing a silver urn.

"Before we open our implement boxes," he said. "I want everyone to take a look at this thing right here. This is a common, everyday… *thing we all use*. It's so common we don't even notice it. Dig?"

Francine raised her hand. "I have absolutely no idea what that is."

"Good people," he said. "This is a… it's what you call a…"

"A samovar," said a man who looked like an older version of John LaZar from *Beyond the Valley of the Dolls*.

"Ladies and gentlemen," Jeffries said. "Please welcome, playing the role of our Tribal Chief and Solar Elder, the talented Mr. John LaZar."

Francine *thought* she'd recognized the guy who played Dr. Jurevicious in *Attack of the 60-Foot Centerfold*, not to mention the freaky hermaphrodite in *Beyond the Valley of the Dolls*.

LaZar bowed to a smattering of applause.

"So, what's a samovar?" Francine asked.

"Okay, whatever," Jeffries said. "I looked all around this place for some kind of simple appliance to demonstrate my point and all I found was this thing in the utility closet with some canisters of mustard gas. Come on, actors. *Pretend* like you know what it is."

Jeffries carried it over to Michelle Skye, a pretty Eurasian who played Queen Labyrinthius in *Jungles of Mars* – a film in which Francine briefly appeared in the role of Gargantua's Companion #1. And it would figure she was here: Every time Francine felt like she had a shot at a leading role, or even a big role, she'd walk into the audition waiting room and there'd be Michelle, confident and looking like she'd had a six-hour makeover, giving that sympathetic smile that said, *sorry to disappoint you once again*.

Barely moving her head, Michelle glanced at the urn.

"From now on," Jeffries said. "When you see something like this, I want you to reach like a hunter-gatherer from the late Pleistocene..." he checked an index card in his pocket, "... early Holocene period in North America. You have never *seen* a Mr. Coffee, never *seen* a Quasar microwave oven. Got me? So, everyone practice looking at everyday things like you've never seen them before."

Everyone started looking around the room.

"In your spare time," Jeffries said. "Spare time."

"Well, what *have* we seen?" an older man asked. "Just dirt and wolves and pheasants?" Francine didn't recognize the frosty-haired man with a slight resemblance to *Tic-Tac-Dough*'s Wink Martindale.

"Negative on the pheasants, Hunstiber. Everybody look in your boxes. There's a list of animals you hunt and some experiences you may have had."

"Meat and hide preservation?" Michelle read aloud.

"In order to survive the winter, it is essential that the women learn how to skin animals and dry the meat while the men are hunting additional meat. The name of your tribe is Uhluk. No real meaning there, but it's a simple sound – *guttural*. You're a nomadic, hunter-gatherer tribe – non-agrarian, though you get wheat germ and stuff from emissaries who return from the Great Plains every other solstice. You can make weapons and carve tools and start a fire, but developmentally you are all over the place; not trading in slaves or meat or handiwork or anything, eating what you hunt, wearing what you weave. Hand-to-mouth. You have a Tribal Chief – played by Mr. LaZar – and a holy man – Hunstiber – but these leaders are mostly ceremonial, and do not reap any particular *spoils*. 'Kay? Everybody shares. Nobody accumulates possessions, except for little totems and stuff. Therefore, you are *ripe* to be taught the ways of civilization and competition that are going to guarantee your survival as a race. That's in your blood, people: the desire to stay alive and procreate and occasionally express yourself.

"Now, in the boxes you'll find everyday gear. Hunters, you've got flint for fire – you'll have to find your own bison dung for kindling – a flint borer for chipping, slingshots and stone carrying pouches – please practice as far as possible from the animal cages – deer-antler picks for digging dirt and extracting meat from the hot coals, a perforated antler – I have no idea what that's for – and several little stone-carved animal heads you may use as spiritual devices. One of you may even have a carved mammoth tusk."

Roanoke Sonoma, a slightly hunky guy with a Harry Hamlin dimple, waved the tusk to a smattering of applause.

"Many thanks to Doniphan. He carved those by hand."

"Thank you, Mr. Jeffries," Doniphan said. "By the way, anyone who wants to keep their unique, hand-carved idols as set souvenirs when this wraps, they're fifty bucks a piece, two for seventy-five."

James McElroy, another die-hard from the audition circuit, held up his totem, a kind of squat little thing with horns. 'What's this supposed to be?"

"A woolly mountain goat," Doniphan said. "Good milkers. Now, three actors don't have caveman gear. Nicholas Boon, Ryan Konner and Alfonse Leroux. You guys are playing the astronauts. So, you might as well go and get your radiation meters and start practicing outside."

"Women," Jeffries continued. "Most of you have dried wattles, nettles and lichen balls in your box. Listen up when I say *hold onto those nettles!* If for any reason you have to take refuge in a cave, they make good insulation. Under those you'll find something like a little wicker God's Eye – that's the beginning of your first basket. Gonna weave about forty of those by the end of next week, so get a feel for them. In addition, you'll find sharp flints for skinning hides, leather water sacks and a little stone bowl… plus a chalk lamp bowl and beading material if you want to make a necklace. Not mandatory."

"I wish *we* got carved animals," Gail said. "I really love animals."

"Not enough to go around for the squaws, I'm afraid. You can borrow your Male Possessor's animal if he gives you the A-okay."

"Um," Francine said. "I don't know my Male Possessor."

"What's it say on your character card?"

"Beyzore."

"I'm Beyzore," Roanoke, the guy with the Harry Hamlin chin, said. Two beats and Francine had it: Lieutenant Rucker Davis III from *Indecent Explosions*, plus two seasons as Corey Carmichael on daytime's *Faithless*. Damn, she was good.

Jeffries said, "Beyzore, meet Luhk, your bitch."

Francine, speechless, looked at Michelle, who rolled her eyes.

"People," he continued, "this is no place for politics. We are the Uhluk, a patriarchal tribe with a zero-tolerance policy when it comes to morality, equality and enlightenment. Our females weave, whittle, have sex, make children and skin meat. And that's cool."

"And what *about* that meat," Michelle said.

"It's all cool. Next week, a local taxidermist is going to demonstrate how to skin a carcass." Jeffries flipped through his papers. "Oh, and Dr. Cameron Chapman – a linguist from UNLV – will be here next week to teach you a basic, unique language and a vocabulary of hand gestures."

"No English?" Hunstiber asked.

"Homeboy, you people don't even know how to grow corn yet. Hey – that reminds me – who's a weaver in here?"

Francine, Gail and Aloe Manuel – a recently defected Mexican soap star – raised their hands.

"A U.S. Textile Museum curator is coming with a kick-ass loom to pass along some primitive weaving techniques. And what about concubines?"

Three demure women waved from the corner.

"Melanie, Stacey and Ronda… your body ornaments get

glued the Sunday before principal photography. Oh, and nobody showers."

Everyone moaned.

"Going for accuracy here. You can sponge off at the creek if you want."

"There's no creek," Doniphan said.

"Like I said, no showers."

"What's the deal," Francine asked, "with the blue paint?"

"Non-concubine women under 8,000 Solar Revs are naked from the waist-up except for a thin coat of clay and charcoal mix that looks a tad blue."

"See…" Francine squeezed her temples.

Doniphan leaned in and said, "I sort of mentioned her before, Mr. Jeffries."

"Any strong feelings, actors?" Jeffries called out.

"What are the men wearing," Michelle Skye asked, "…down there?"

Jeffries blinked. "Muslin-lined Bison skin."

"Concealed completely?"

"What did I just--" Jeffries grabbed his hair. "This is all anthropologically accurate. Back at this time--"

"No, no, no," Michelle said, "I bet that if you went back in time you'd see penises flapping all over the place."

"No, you wouldn't."

"They didn't have muslin, that's for sure."

"Well…" Jeffries let go of his Afro, leaving handprints. "Focus group after focus group has told us moviegoers don't want to see penises flapping all over the place. Not even on public television."

"I thought that this project was for the government?"

"The government doesn't want to see penises, either; they do, however, want to see breasts. And they want the penises hidden from view and calling the shots. Dig?"

"Here's the deal." Francine said. "I'll weave baskets. I'll dry meat. I'll let Beyzore drag me by the hair and simulate prehistoric nookie. But, I refuse – repeat – *refuse* to have my boobs painted blue."

"Defy me on this issue and I have no choice but to recast your ass."

"Fine."

"Okay." Jeffries thought a moment. "From here on out you will be known as the Buzzard Keeper!"

"Swell," Francine said.

"A hermit, an outcast, a collector of molds--"

"I'm already growing real attached to these nettles."

"--shunned from society, ridiculed, misunderstood, your only friends the turkey vultures and an occasional glyptodon tortoise. You will live in a meager lean-to on the outskirts of the valley, constantly subjected to the elements and the harassment of the male hunters."

"Hello?" Roanoke waved. "What about my character, Beyzore? She's supposed to clean my hut and stuff."

"Donnie?" Jeffries turned to his assistant. "Thoughts?"

After a moment, Doniphan said, "Luhk ignored the tribal laws and was made outcast."

"Yesss," Jeffries hissed, pointing at the ceiling.

"But she's still Beyzore's woman. So, unbeknownst to the tribe, he visits her every evening with offerings of smilodon meat and water and fetish paraphernalia from his travels – feathers, bones, etc. In addition, he protects her from the lustful males and scornful females."

"I don't need Beyzore," Francine said. "I can protect myself."

"Believe me," Doniphan said. "It'll create an irresistible romantic pathos."

"Sold!" Jeffries high-fived his assistant. "Now, everybody break out your personalized totems."

viii.

Sharise Vanderslice was arranging her naked Star Trek figurines on the Transporter diorama, when she sensed ghostly silhouettes in her office doorway. "You crazy kids," she said, sighing, as her eyes adjusted to her beloved niece and nephew, who were wearing matching mock turtlenecks and gray flannels

Sharise, a youthful forty-five with a hairstyle that hadn't had a refresh since *Hands Across America*, was Goddard's chief Rocket Science engineer, a NASA fixture who had declined many opportunities – and requests – to retire, since joining the program as an Apollo 14 intern out of M.I.T.

"Come on in," she said. "Come play with my toys... just like the old days."

Travis and Mabel Mountjoy took in the spectacle of their aunt, who wore a hand-embroidered, magenta caftan with silver bangles on each wrist; and her office, with the life-size Grays sitting cross-legged in the corner, model spaceships hanging from the ceiling on fishing line, figurines of wizards and goblins and medieval warriors, and movie posters for *It Came From Outer Space*, *Forbidden Planet* and *On Golden Pond*.

"I *wish* we could play, Aunt Sharise," Mabel said. "We're here on official business."

Mabel slumped in a chair while Travis lingered at a hanging

photo triptych of Sharise dressed as a Renaissance-era bar wench, Queen Elizabeth I and Ming the Merciless, respectively.

"Aunt Sharise, as you know, Travis and I are running CHETO division."

"I saw the internal memo. Congratulations. If you don't mind my asking, how do two teenagers pull that kind of thing off?"

"Well, we're fully qualified astro-physicists, Aunt Sharise," Mabel said. "We've basically been doing Dad's job the last few years. Anyway, when he died we inherited CHETO's private endowment and that puts us in charge."

"So why don't you guys spend the summer on a party boat in Greece or something?"

"We have a dream to fulfill."

Travis leaned in. "And we want to see VITRIOL."

"What, may I ask, does CHETO want with that? It's a dead project."

"Dormant," Travis said, "not dead."

"Dead as dirt. VITRIOL won't pass prototype stage for another hundred years." She held out a bowl of Ginger candy. "We just don't have the funding."

Mabel took some ginger candy and tossed one to Travis.

"I mean, don't get me started," Sharise said. "Administrator Chilblain has been telling us in straight ways and subtle that the current administration won't even approve on our most *modest* deep space projects; meanwhile, he hasn't done a darn thing to educate the public on what we're capable of achieving this very day. Nobody cares! Nowadays, it's all about getting satellite views of what's down here. Glacier movements, hurricanes, earthquakes. Me, me, me!"

The twins, chewing, nodded respectfully.

"If John Doe realized the implications of the Mars Rover

finding fungus spores on the Ascraeus Mons Volcano, we'd be flush. But VITRIOL… Oh, boy, this can work. It will work. Someday. When I'm dead and gone."

"How about right now?" Travis asked.

"Don't kid."

"You know," he said, "CHETO has been receiving private endowments for over fifty years, but we've been sitting on our hands that whole time, spending nothing, waiting for… well, aliens."

"I hear ya."

"Congress scoffs at us, the White House won't meet with us and NASA is becoming so salt-of-the-earth, before long we're all going to be handing out warm towel-ettes on chartered orbit shuttles. Long story short, Aunt Sharise, we're sitting on a shit-load of use-it-or-lose-it cash."

Mabel leaned closer. "And we want to use VITRIOL spacecraft in a top-secret experiment to make sure we don't lose this endowment in the NASA budget appropriations."

"I can't believe what I'm hearing."

"Don't feel the need to decide now," Travis said.

"But understand," Mabel said, "if you say no we're going over your head."

"This is stunning. You mean to say… if I hear this right… Are you talking mission-level endeavor? Mars? Jupiter? Beyond?"

The twins got up and Mabel said, "I think we better go have a look at this machine."

•••

A shaft of hazy light cut through the dark hangar. A loud clap followed as the overhead lights fell on a large, shrouded object in the center. The motorized lever pulled away the shroud and the twins, like pilgrims, approached VITRIOL: NASA's towering prototype for interstellar travel.

"It almost looks like a flower," Mabel said.

Three cone-shaped boosters connecting to the main hull by steel beams – each crowned with a ring of fuel tanks – formed the base of the craft. Radiator vanes above the middle booster led to the main octagonal reactor, then to a long tubular duct that mounted a broad, web-like funnel at the top, open to the sky like a gigantic rain gauge.

"Wow." Mabel walked under the right-hand booster. "Hydrogen powered?"

"Correct."

Travis pulled out a sketchpad. "And where's the fuel storage?"

"That's the miracle of VITRIOL. The days of lugging huge fuel tanks are over. Once the Initial Propellant System is engaged, the craft can reach ram speeds, making it possible for that big scoop up there to seek fuel-rich fields in space, intake the ionized hydrogen, pull it into the main duct…" She pointed to the tubular middle section… "…through the generator, second-level duct, gas accelerator, into the reactor and *boom*."

"Boom," Travis said, dreamily. "It thrives on the elements. Sweet."

"Where do the people go?" Mabel asked.

"The people?"

"Yeah, like the astronauts."

"Hmm. Remember, VITRIOL was conceived as an unmanned probe. It is – to be frank – a solitary, violent engine. You see there… that's a genuine fusion reactor. We would have to create highly durable radiation shields to house crew modules and Landers."

Without taking his eyes off his sister, Travis said, "How long would that take?"

"You mean implementing command, accommodation and recreation modules with a services core that operates the craft's propulsion reactors?"

The twins, locked in a stare, said, "Sure."

"What are we talking about here, kids? Come on, spill it."

Mabel tapped the electron beam generators with a pencil. "How much cashola to get this thing cranked up?"

"Fully functional? Sheesh… When I shut down the project a few years ago, I estimated around $900 billion. Today, I don't know. Inflation."

"Okay," Travis said. "Here's what I'm thinking… Sharise, you're getting on in years--"

"Mister Mountjoy!"

"No, no. Hear me out, Aunt Sharise. You are *never* going to see this thing get off the ground. And even a hundred years and a trillion dollars from now, who's to say something better won't come along or whether anyone will care? It's the same thing we're facing at CHETO. Mabel and I have worked since we were in accelerated Montessori to try and fulfill our grandfather's dreams of mankind coming face-to-face with extra-terrestrials."

"With the proper protocol," Mabel said.

"With the proper protocol. However, our poor father – your brother – failed to get men into deep space to find aliens and then he died and here we are left with the bag."

"I know, I know," Sharise said, catching a tear. "But what does this have to do with me getting on in years?"

"Aren't you curious to know how a human would *react* to meeting an alien? Think about the confusion, the fear, the awkwardness. I mean, that's all you're getting at here with VITRIOL. Am I right? All of us in this business want to see *who's* out there much more than what. But, our organization, our government, our public don't seem to care about that anymore – except in movies – because we haven't delivered jack squat. Let's be honest: Research is all we do."

Sharise said, "Don't forget S.E.T.I. They're proactive."

"They listen to radio static all day. Hello? Aliens do not have radios. See what I'm saying? We're just pushing the knowledge a little further down the line for someone else to pick up."

"It's true." Sharise sniffed. "I feel so alone sometimes."

"And maybe… *maybe* we can help future generations prepare for alien encounters by doing extensive research on our own astronauts first."

"I guess when you're talking about humans meeting aliens that's half your research there," Sharise said. "The astronauts."

"Exactly. And it's budget-friendly."

Mabel waved Travis over to inspect the strap-on pulse boosters, leaving Sharise with a moment to gaze at her towering spacecraft. Again she was reminded how cheerlessly it sat every day under wraps – like the scooters and skates left in far-flung corners of her garage when she went away to college – and how she secretly ached for this enormous hunk of junk, hoping and praying for it to see sunlight, to show the world its awesome capabilities. The VITRIOL was the lynch pin of her career, and the only reason she stuck around Goddard anymore. Sure, she got to work on the first few Mars probes, which were fun – and she still got the chills thinking about the Ascraeus Mons fungus spores – but nothing could compare with her intense VITRIOL fantasies, as she plowed through space like a krill-sucking whale, propelled by the swirling elements, hanging onto the edge of the scoop funnel with the wind in her hair and the majestic endlessness sparkling before her in a panoramic paradise.

ix.

Francine climbed out of the Cave. The sky, with towering columns of cloud, arched like a protective dome over the mile-wide valley. In the distance, the pole-and-thatch crew were bending birch limbs covered with mangy animal hides, while across the clearing a camera crew mounted sun-shades and set frame-lines with microphone booms that dipped like fishing poles. Over by a large group of tents she could see trailers and animal cages, portable toilets, and a helicopter; and along the valley cliffs, guys in cherry pickers made cave-size holes with boring drills and sledgehammers, while associate producers leaned rickety birch ladders alongside them.

Francine chewed gum and wandered east toward a chain-link fence that encircled a herd of seriously hairy yaks. Suddenly an explosion rocked the canyon and a cloud blackened against the sky. Cheers followed from the pole-and-thatch crews. Francine kept on for another hundred yards until she came upon a long trench.

"Hey," she called into the pit.

Two grimy guys, trying to extract a muddy rock, leaned against the edge.

"Gum?"

They both took some.

"What is this?"

"A barrow."

"Cool. A barrow?"

"An ancient burial mound."

"Very cool."

"Gotta finish so we can sand the altar."

"Nice to meet you," she said, and continued on to a forklift holding two fifteen-foot-long stones. She was running her hands along the coarse, scalloped surfaces when something grabbed her fingers.

"Shit fuck!" she was saying, when the visor-pinched Afro popped up. "Jesus H., Jeffries."

He hopped up on the rock. "Sorry I lost my cool back there in the kick-off meeting," he said. "Just gotta show who's boss."

"I guess." Francine walked away, toward the large tents.

"Baby, what's gotten into you?" He followed.

"Well," she said, "I'm not a little nitwit anymore. I'm thirty."

"Bullshit. You're an actor. You can be anybody, do anything, *wear* anything. Or nothing. And that's okay."

"Damnit, Jeffries. Look at me. Who's going to hire me in ten years if I keep doing this shit?"

"Girl, this ain't *Donahue*. There's no shame and humility. It's about staying in character. And your character doesn't care about how she looks. In fact… " Jeffries put on his glasses, opening a notebook. "Your character has lived a 'life of servitude,' with 'beatings and humiliations,' married to a man in denial of his own reproductive dysfunctionality." He flipped a page. "She spends all day weaving leg wraps and peeling the skin off bloody bison carcasses and doesn't give two shits about her painted-blue boobs hanging out all over the place."

"Funny," she said. "This reminds me of the first time I did a nude scene."

"You never forget."

"*Hell Beach*. I was Surfer Chick #3 – no man's land – but the director wanted someone topless and they picked me. I was like, *I don't know about this*. Didn't feel like a privilege. I mean, I was eighteen and this means I can't invite my grandfather to the premiere."

"Which is cool."

"So, the director said, 'It will be empowering.' I was hesitant. He told me, 'It will get your name out there.' I was skeptical. He told me, 'Get off the set.' So, I took off my top and sat on a towel for three hours while they doused me with a plant sprayer so I'd glisten."

Another explosion went off in the distance and Jeffries whipped out his pocket binoculars. "Thirty films later…" he said, adjusting the zoom wheel.

"Yeah, nothing. It's gotten me dead-end roles, time after time. Never a lead. And it's ruined my personal life. Years go by and I attract the wrong kind of men. People from the shoot, usually; things get kinky and then you realize you're living in some guy's mixed-up fantasy world."

Jeffries sniffed. "Men," he said, putting away the binoculars. "But this is something bigger."

They came to one of the large tents, flapping tightly in the wind.

"You directors never work harder than when you're trying to convince some girl to get naked."

A long, curved tusk slipped out of the tent and bumped Francine.

"What the…" She opened the flap. An elephant stood patiently while several prop techs pulled nylons over its legs.

"Excuse me." Two women carrying garbage bags filled with

yak hair ducked into the tent. They emptied the bags near a group of people stitching the hair into the nylon material.

Jeffries poked Francine's arm. "Look, do you even want to be here?"

"No choice," she said. "Either I do this or I go to jail."

"So, why not have fun with it?"

"I'm fine being the turkey vulture outcast, like you said. It's the same kind of shit I always do."

"No!" Jeffries yelled, making the elephant rear back a little. "Look, I've got three concubines, three weavers and a sorceress. The first six of those, one way or another, are topless, and I can't have one hulking in one corner of the valley acting all modest."

"Who's the sorceress?"

"I'm thinking Michelle Skye."

"Why not make me Sorceress?"

"Michelle has that Asian thing going on."

"And I got the topless idiot thing going on. See, Jeffries?"

One of the curved elephant tusks fell off, and a guy with a glue gun ran over.

"Girl, I tell you what: Work with me. Keep an open mind. Be a weaver. Be topless. No blue paint until principal photography. We'll close the set. And when we're all done with this… whatever it is, I'll cast you in *Slow Death*."

"Hah." Francine fed the elephant some hay. "Playing some sort of real estate agent stripper, I'm sure."

"Maybe a tight mini-skirt. But you'll get SAG pay scale, residuals and who knows what could happen with that exposure."

Francine stared hard at his quivering eyes. "I'll be in *Slow Death*. Swear?"

He touched his heart, kissed his finger and pointed up.

"No blue paint until Principal?"

He closed his eyes and nodded.

"No spur-of-the-moment tits-and-ass requests?"

"On my honor."

"And I apply my own blue paint."

He stopped nodding. "Um, no can do, baby."

"What? Why?"

"We'll lose our insurance," he said, turning. "Well, speak of the devil, won't you."

Peeking out of a half-constructed beehive hut, the Props woman who'd threatened Francine with the spear pulled out a bamboo chute tube and went *fthew!*

Jeffries stood there laughing hysterically with a toy suction arrow stuck to his forehead.

<u>Senator Tilly:</u> Chief Skin Flayer refers to a Valley of Never-Ending Spite, which is commonly known as the Stribling Valley, part of Shacklett Air Force Base in--

<u>Chief Skin Flayer:</u> If I may interrupt, Senator, the agreement between my tribe and Lt. Colonel Robert Mackey Stribling in 1867 did not transfer complete ownership to the U.S. Government. I have a document here that refers -- and I'm quoting -- to a spiritual retention, with every member of the Meemaw entitled to return to the valley - at the discretion of the agreed ceremonial calendar - for prayer, ceremonial and ritualistic purposes.

<u>Senator Tilly:</u> Well, I appreciate this document. It's a little torn. Let me get my glasses out.

<u>Chief Skin Flayer:</u> It was written on corn shucks. That's why it's in plastic.

<u>Senator Tilly:</u> I appreciate that. Now, let me remind you, Chief Skin Flayer, that we are meeting today to discuss Native American gambling licenses and how they relate to soil subsidies already remunerated to Native American tribal communities, not Stribling Valley. And besides, the valley in question is located within a U.S. Air Force base, which goes well beyond the jurisdiction of this committee… joint committee.

<u>Chief Skin Flayer:</u> Senator, on behalf of the Meemaw, I wish to say that it is upsetting to hear stories, dubious or not, that the Valley of Never-Ending Spite - access to which we have been wrongfully denied for one-hundred and fifty years - might be used for the purposes of [CLASSIFIED. DELETED BY GENERAL CONSENT]

<u>Senator Tilly:</u> I appreciate that, Chief, but not only have we gone beyond the bounds of this joint committee; we may have entered into a discussion of classified matters.

<u>Chief Skin Flayer:</u> Just please stop calling it Stribling Valley.

<u>Senator Tilly:</u> Okay.

– Excerpted from: <u>Hearings on 1988 Soil Subsidies and How They Relate to Tribal Gambling Licenses</u>: Joint Session of the Agriculture and Indian Affairs Committees, U.S. Senate, Dirksen Room 2345, September 26, 1989

X.

Room 4563-T in Goddard's Blue Wing is known as the Safe. It is a room within a room, fully soundproofed and uniquely wired for communications. Though Goddard is a relatively new facility, with a minimum threat of baked-in spy taps, the Safe is guarded and maintained by a retired Air Force officer who performs a security check every evening before setting the alarm system and sealing the room with a combination lock.

Today the officer stood watch in the doorway while Colonel Nimrod T. Ashby, Lt. Colonel Erasmus J.T. Clark and Captain T.W. Tongue sat at the oval conference table in the window-less, wood-paneled room.

Ashby sat in a high-backed leather chair, staring bleary eyed across the room at a framed satellite photo of the United States that showed the most populous energy sectors. *Grids.* The word hung over him.

Beside him, Erasmus Clark spun an anti-gravity pen on the table; on the other side, T.W. Tongue snored, his head on the table, jerking now and then; a listlessness that was the result of their vigorous training the last few weeks, during which they had been awakened at odd hours for intensive human proximity habitability simulations, fructose infusions and the occasional moon rover joyride; each of them sequestered from daylight, transported – blindfolded – from place to place, a method of training that he hoped was part of an overall plan preparing them for... something. But the disorientation, the lack of outside contact and the physical exhaustion had begun to make him feel like he'd been shrunk and stored away and forgotten.

Sitting in that sub-level conference room, they could have been anywhere – in Alabama's Marshall Flight Center, still in Maryland at Goddard, or in Spain's Moròn Air Base, for that matter. It didn't help to wonder. The world had become a small cave, all these locations simply names, words, signs for things that might be renamed hundreds of years later. *Grids*.

A round man in a V-neck sweater bounded into Room 4563-T carrying a stuffed manila folder. After tossing presentation papers to the astronauts, he said to the ceiling, "We're ready." The lights dimmed and a flat-screen panel lowered on the wall. A ceiling projector glowed, displaying the image of a green planet sectioned with latitude lines.

"Greetings," the man said. "My name is Frank Delaplane. I am a Planet Watcher from the University of Cheyenne." He tossed his business cards across the table. "I am here to brief you on the discovery of a planet in another solar system that is close – possibly the closest ever found – to the size and nature of Earth."

Erasmus Clark watched as, on the projector, the animated green planet merged with a diagram of the Earth, the sight of which made him dizzy: somehow, based on his intense quarantine, he believed that he had already left the Earth. Seeing it again made him feel stuck in a prolonged, uncomfortable farewell.

The Planet Watcher continued, "This planet, in the U Majoris Galaxy, named 47 U Maj D based on pre-existing naming conventions, is unique among all the others in that it quite *possibly* could have a rocky surface, an essential platform for life."

"For life to evolve, Mr. Delaplane?" Clark asked.

"Well, yes. The evolution of life."

"So your focus is on the discovery or potential of life, as opposed to finding habitable planets?"

"We do both, sir."

"Understood. I guess I'm just wondering… We've been… I just want to know whether we're talking about actually *finding* life… or if this is just about a planet that's going to be colonized."

"We must first establish whether or not there is the potential for life," Delaplane replied, "before even considering colonization." He clicked the remote. "This is a very new science, you see."

The next graphic showed a powerful light telescope sending a beam to a planet. "Planets, as you know, do not give off light," he said. "They merely reflect the stars they orbit. Therefore, because no planet outside our solar system – not even using the most powerful telescope – is visible to the naked eye, we detect a planet's size by measuring changes in the light emitted by a single star while the planet revolves around it." A video graphic showed a planet eclipsing a star, slowly blocking out the light. "Composition detection is mainly a matter of speculation."

Clark said, "What was that again?"

"Composition detection – for instance, whether or not there's a rocky surface – is principally a matter of speculation. What I mean by that is, to date, we have predominately found large gaseous planets, which formulate away from a star and migrate toward it over time, growing more gaseous." The projector showed a brief animated video of a spinning planet – like Jupiter, with blurry green and red stripes. "However, a smaller planet found closer to a star *likely* formed much closer to the star and is most *probably* rocky."

A loud snore erupted. Ashby reached over to shake Captain

Tongue, he woke and stared at the screen with the image of a gleaming star with a mass of rock orbiting it and slowly becoming a ball, as if invisible hands were molding it.

"Now, as I said…." Delaplane stacked his papers crisply. "47 U Maj D is probably rocky. There is no way, at this point, to tell for sure. What we do know is that the planet in question is orbiting a star that lives 35 light-years from Earth in the direction of the Cancer constellation – relatively close. The planet is slightly larger than Earth."

Clark raised his hand. "If it is *like* Earth, with rocks and water, how do we speculate the compatibility for life? Can you measure its evolution in geographical development and gauge from there whether or not life is beginning to germinate or will someday?"

"Toughie," Delaplane said. "We can measure the distance it orbits a star to see if it has a lukewarm zone. Planets can't be too hot or cold. After that it's hard to say. I mean, a young planet could still be ahead of the evolution curve based on circumstances… or it could be years behind or non-capable, based on the amount of radiation retained on the surface…. I guess what I'm asking out loud is, is there a definitive result of occurrences having to do with physics and chemistry and geography that spawned life as we know it on Earth?" Delaplane shrugged. "Or, are we – you and me, us, here – the result of some miracle; maybe some divine--"

"That'll be all, Frank." Travis Mountjoy stood in the doorway holding a small wooden box; his sister Mabel was behind him, her face firm but placid.

Delaplane quickly gathered his papers and ducked out of the room.

Travis and Mabel shut the door. They sat down across from

the astronauts.

"So what did you guys think of that?" Travis asked, popping his knuckles.

Ashby glanced at his fellow astronauts. "Well, I knew there were research crews scouting potential planets, but I didn't know about this one."

"No one knows about this one," Mabel said.

"Listen, let me make one thing clear," Travis continued. "Mr. Delaplane may have discovered this planet, but forget what he said about the *probabilities*. Little people live in a world of probabilities. We don't."

Mabel shut off the projector. "Presentation over," she said to the room. The lights came on. Everyone blinked. "Gentlemen, we're going to explain why you're here; why you've been quarantined, sequestered and what this planet has to do with it.

"After Mr. Deleplane's team discovered 47 U Maj D, the planet underwent close examination with one of our classified, deep-space telescopes. Infrared imaging proved not only that it has a lukewarm zone, optimally distant from a star; not only that it is relatively free of radiation, but that it is 67-percent water-based and is following a trajectory pattern of geographical evolution perfectly parallel to Earth."

T.W. Tongue coughed. "Are you serious?"

"Why wouldn't we be serious?"

"A parallel universe?"

Colonel Clark turned to him. "Well, think about it, Captain. There are billions... I mean, why wouldn't there be?"

Travis moved the wooden box, arbitrarily, a few inches to the right. "Gentlemen, this planet is following the Earth's trajectory of development, but is, we calculate, 8,000 years behind us in sophistication."

Tongue swiveled in his chair, stretched and yawned. "So they're just now airing 'Battle of the Network Stars'."

Ashby said, "8,000 years?"

"Three years ago," Travis said, "we sent an unmanned probe to orbit the U Majoris. Last year we received a file with aerial images of 47 U Maj D, showing what we believe are multi-cellular human organisms living in a primitive society almost identical to that of the late Pleistocene, early Holocene period in North America."

The men sat staring in different directions; and for a short time, the only sound was Travis tapping a Dunhill lighter on the table.

"Gentlemen," Mabel said. "I know this is hard to take in all at once."

Ashby stared at the polished wood of the table, while Clark ground his teeth and Tongue scratched his stubbly neck.

"Though we'd like to offer you access to a spiritual adviser to guide you through any philosophical conundrums, you signed the waiver and everything so we don't have to. This is just *way* too classified. Nevertheless, a lot of questions may be forming that could interfere with the integrity of the mission. We can't *say* whether or not human life is in abundance in the universe, and we can't *comment* on whether or not our similarities to these creatures indicate a higher intelligence at work. But what we can understand together, with pride, is that each of you have sacrificed your lives on Earth to embark into the unknown, to join us on an unprecedented endeavor of mind-blowing discovery and we really appreciate it!"

Travis opened the wooden box. "Cuban Hoyo des Dieux, gentlemen. Finest in the world."

xi.

The actors, irritable after a week without soap, deodorant or cosmetics, gathered in the valley for another Body Endurance course, while the setting sun hurled stolid currents everywhere, dissolving against the sky like a watery pill.

Francine kicked back on the wicker pad and watched the others stretch, the men in sweats and T-shirts – except for Hunstiber, who wore a low-neck leotard that displayed a shrub of red chest hair – the ladies in spandex, drawstring pants and tanks, except for Francine herself, who wore a cut-off jean skirt with ankle-high tights and a T-shirt that said, "Stop Looking at My Ass," on the back.

In the foreground, Doniphan arranged lance-heads, deer-antlers, stone sickles and other implements on a red and black Navajo blanket. Behind him a leopard tortoise scraped along. And somewhere above the valley rim, the restless mammoths screeched – a call answered by the yaks in the pens below.

Everyone, at once, sensed the calm. The jackhammers, after four straight days of rattling, had stopped; and the production teams, after touching up the burial mounds, beehives and stone altar, had left the scene. The animal trainer's Air Stream had been hauled away with most of the white tents, and the dolly of leftover birch poles and stacks of bison hides fished out by a helicopter. No unnatural sound could be heard, except for the wind-tunnel fans drying the sandstone boulders freshly painted with primitive hieroglyphics.

Francine, lazily stretching her hamstring, watched Jeffries climb out of the Jarlsburg Butte Cave, swinging his bullhorn.

"Uhluk Tribe!" he said. "Give your attention to Hunstiber Reed. As some of you know, Mr. Reed owns and operates Silent Knights, the second largest mime school in the country. He's gonna kick-off our workshop with a basic body-language demo."

Francine glanced at Michelle, who was making a blowjob hand gesture.

Hunstiber, now in the foreground, said, "Tribesmen and tribeswomen, this is all about discovering your low center of gravity." He then proceeded to chicken-walk around the exercise pad.

Jeffries' bullhorn cracked. "According to my recent studies, Pleistocene man, while not hunched like the Neanderthal, still kept a *low center of gravity* for efficiency in hunting and defense."

Hunstiber waved. "Follow me 'round the quicksand pool!"

In a big line, everyone chicken-walked toward a muddy pit. Michelle, behind Gail, yanked her shorts. Gail screamed "No!" even though she had spandex underneath. Tears followed, and Michelle pulled her out of line for a hug.

When the group returned they found, standing next to Jeffries, a sort of cross between William Hurt and John Hurt in pleated khakis. He was holding a spear with a scorched-black tip.

"Nice work, people." Jeffries applauded. "Now please turn your attention to Professor Cameron Chapman of UNLV, who is here to demonstrate several *primal* body mechanisms."

Chapman, scowling, thrust his spear to the left, right, over his head, his jaw buzzing like an angry guinea pig. He dropped the spear and said, "This is known as a Threat Display."

Suddenly, a shriek came from the middle of the valley, and Francine turned to see a full-grown Bengal tiger leap from the animal tent with a single, seven-inch-long incisor sticking out of its mouth. Following him were three wranglers carrying rifles.

The tiger burned past the yaks, leapt over the barrow mound, and made for the surface road.

On the cliff above, a white Bronco II skidded to a stop. Two men hopped out and aimed scoped rifles at the tiger, now sprinting up the incline.

The wranglers in the valley waved. "Hold Fire!" One knelt, aimed low and took a dust shot. The next dart hit. The tiger collapsed, sliding hard against the road, and rolled over, his belly shining white.

The wranglers hoisted the creature onto a stretcher and immediately glued another saber-tooth to the opposite incisor.

"Fun's over!" Jeffries' bullhorn blared.

Dr. Chapman fished a hairy mannequin head out of his satchel. "Now, everyone find a buddy and I'll demonstrate the three fundamentals of de-lousing."

xii.

Before dawn the next morning Jeffries and Doniphan strolled through the gravely dusk with the *Operation EMU* script.

"'Aliens Land at Night,'" Doniphan read.

Jeffries lowered his binoculars. "FX makes the call."

"That's scene twelve. Hope we can maintain interest."

"We'll put the transporter there." Jeffries pointed. "So, they're trapped. Jarlsburg Cavern there, thatch village there."

The grub truck beeped fifty yards away, backing into the catering tent, and people began to unload thermoses and cellophane-covered platters.

"Bear claw?" Jeffries asked.

"Cruller man myself."

They strolled towards the tent, swatting at the day's first gnats.

"Mr. Jeffries, I have a few questions."

"Shoot."

"We open with the new Tribal Elder burying the old Tribal Elder. John LaZar is our new Tribal Elder. Who's our old one?"

"We'll get some wonk from the Air Force base; you know, lay him out with his favorite hunting arrows, then light the funeral pyre and cut to the concubine dance sequence."

"What about the burial mound?"

"Oh, right. Forget the pyre. Props will make a covered corpse and we'll stuff him in there. Next question."

Doniphan lifted the catering tent flap. "What do we shoot first?"

They came upon two long tables arranged with pastries, bowls of fruit, coffee and bottled water.

"Decided that just now." Jeffries pumped the thermos. "We'll rehearse 'Uhluk Tribe Meets the Aliens' first thing next week, full dress, no cameras. I want the first unit filming a handful of extras by the pole-and-thatches, making fire, carving, delousing, squabbling."

"Storyboards?"

"Pending."

They ducked out into the purple dawn.

"I love this time of day," Jeffries said. "When you feel like you have the world to yourself for a moment."

"I prefer the hours between midnight and two. When it feels like amazing and unusual things are erupting everywhere."

"Donnie, that's the time of day where people think stupid and act stupid."

"Doniphan, sir."

"Here, check this out."

They stood behind a moving truck. Jeffries unlocked the clamp and slid the hatch upwards. Two Belgian 'Tiger' Squadron helmets rolled out. "Brush those off will you, Donnie?"

"Why is this familiar?"

"*Jungles of Mars.*"

They climbed inside and Jeffries grabbed a first-aid beam and shined it upon what appeared to be a cross between an Air Stream and the car in *Chitty-Chitty Bang-Bang*.

"Didn't recognize it."

"Also used it in *Rescue From the Martian Harem.*" Jeffries

tapped an old switchboard box, "Someone needs to fix this fuel tank contraption."

Doniphan peeked inside at the transporter's lounge area, complete with joystick chess tables, Eames chairs and a wet bar.

"We'll CGI the landing," Jeffries said, "use handhelds for the interior shots. These," he tugged on an orange jumpsuit, "are genuine, L.A. County Department of Transportation highway worker suits. Props will make them space-like."

"So it's *not* aliens landing on this planet. They're humans."

"Yes. Human aliens."

They closed down the truck and headed towards the Props workstations, where several Props techs were working on foldout banquet tables covered in brown paper.

"Jeffries," Doniphan said. "I want to pose a problem."

"Hit me."

"People want to see the script."

"People?"

"Talent. It's been three weeks; body language courses, anthropology, archeology, slingshot practice. I'm just saying…"

"They'll know soon enough."

At one of the Props tables, prosthetic technicians were using fine brushes and dusting cloths to prepare a large collection of scraggly, over-bite dentures.

"What *do* we know, boss? I mean, seriously."

Jeffries popped in a pair of dentures and smiled.

"Look at the script." Doniphan flipped the pages.

Jeffries nodded, trying to remove the dentures.

"After tons of useless exposition having to do with this hunter-gatherer tribe, it ends abruptly after the Gift Exchange sequence."

Two prosthetic technicians had come around the table and

were now trying to help dislodge the teeth from Jeffries' mouth.

"What I'm saying is, we got everybody out here: Actors, costumes, cameras; we even have fifteen dead elk in the freezer truck. And…? For…?"

His mouth freed, Jeffries said, "Do you remember at the very end of *Psycho*--"

"No."

"Just listen, Chief…. At the very end when Vera Miles goes into the cellar and finds Mrs. Bates' corpse in the chair, and Anthony Perkins busts in wearing a summer dress just as John Gavin hooks him from behind and the light bulb swings and the knife falls and the wig comes off and everyone screams?"

"No, I don't." Doniphan scratched his neck and looked away.

"I find that very hard to believe, Donnie. Anyway, Hitchcock didn't let anyone see that script except for little snippets at the appropriate times, and no one -- I repeat, *no one* -- knew the ending until the very last day of shooting."

"I'm sorry. I never saw it."

"Well, that's what I'm talking about." Jeffries grabbed his coffee off the table. "Now, let's go get an update on the saber-tooth tiger situation."

xiii.

NASA Administrator Hank Chilblain, a medium-sized man with striped suspenders, leaned over his desk – a plank made of glass, bare except for a cell phone, a small daily schedule card and a manila folder. He saluted. "That'll be all, Sergeant."

Officer Lee Harriman, steward of Goddard's Room 4563-T, released the Mountjoy Twins, saluted and shut the door behind him.

"Sit down, kids." Chilblain gestured to a set of metal chairs. "You know I had to call NORAD."

"Sorry, sir," Mabel said.

"They were winding up two Apaches to secure our airspace."

"Sir," Travis said. "I had no idea they made such a fuss over smoke alarms."

"I wasn't privy to the Cuban cigars, sir."

"*Not* Cubans," Travis pointed at his sister. "Swisher Sweets with the tips pulled off."

"Listen up, you guys," Chilblain said. "Two days ago, I received an escalation from the Blue Wing Infirmary reporting abuse to astronauts-in-training, in the name of some project I haven't authorized." Chilblain tapped the manila folder. "*Operation EMU*? Come on, kids. What would your dad say?"

Travis inhaled sharply. "Since when, Mr. Administrator, does CHETO branch need sign-off on a private endowment project?"

"Come over here." Chilblain waved them to the window, where they looked across a stretch of woodlands that encircled the suburban patch of Greenbelt, Maryland. "Your father was an extremely interesting man. And he raised you admirably. He and I go *way* back. How did he die again, if you don't mind me asking?"

"That primate infantry experiment for Department of Defense," Mabel said, slouching.

"Thank God that got axed. What happened to the baboons again?"

"Friend Lee's Animal Sanctuary in Ft. Davis, Texas."

"Very civil. Not their fault. You don't give a paintball gun – or any kind of gun, for that matter – to a wild animal. And here's my point: Things like that give CHETO a bad name and lead to *my* higher-ups asking me why a sub-branch of NASA has so much unchecked capital. When they ask who's in charge and I say it's a couple of teenagers – albeit geniuses…. Needless to say, I get tired of defending it. Now, back to the file," he said, returning to his desk. "Okay. Here we go. One of the first things I see here in this report is VITRIOL."

"Sweet machine, sir." Travis said. "Runs without fuel storage."

"I killed it three years ago."

"Yeah, I heard that."

"Which is just one of the many, many problems I see here. For instance, it says here your target planet is nearly identical to Earth with human-like personages."

"I don't think we used the word *personage* exactly."

"Do you kids know how religious people have gotten lately?"

The twins said nothing at first. Then Mabel said, "So?"

Chilblain smiled, bemused. "Part of why I'm so excited here

every day at NASA is that we're looking up, we're not backing down and most importantly we're avoiding serious political controversy. For some reason or another, people out there in our great country – educated people with money, no less – have gotten, well, spiritual. And we have to be sure that none of our space endeavors, experimental or not, tread upon any religious doctrines."

"How would they, sir?"

"What happens when word gets out that we're training astronauts to commiserate with prehistoric humans on an Earth-like planet?"

Mabel bobbed her crossed leg. Travis stretched his neck.

"Let me quote here…. *one of the main objectives being to observe if the subjects nurture development of a subspecies.* And then further down we have…. *if subjects use superior intelligence to take advantage of said sub-species.* What you guys have to ask yourselves, as space-faring individuals, probing the heavenly fabric, is, *what is God's design?*

Travis said, "Want to know how I feel about this, Mr. Administrator?"

"Very much so."

"I think I'm going to hurl."

Mabel said, "I sort of see what you're getting at, sir. Like, the Voyager capsule carried tidbits of human achievement like Bach recordings and Da Vinci sketches, in case aliens ever picked it apart. But, you know, our planet has seven major religions. How do we settle on a doctrine?"

"Methodist," Chilblain said. "That's the one."

"Mr. Administrator." Travis pressed his temples, "I'm afraid we don't have the bandwidth for this conversation."

"Kids, how is this any different from Christopher Columbus?"

"He was a terrorist."

"Come on. When the great ships left Spain with the intention of colonizing the indigenous peoples of America, or Belize or wherever, they came bearing the fruits of religion. Lest you forget, Queen Victoria had strong ties with the Catholic Church and was obliged to send a missionary."

"Queen Isabella," Mabel said.

"And that's fine, but the main point is, picture me in a cabinet meeting – and God forbid this *Operation EMU* winds up on the agenda – and we've got astronauts born, bred and trained in the United States of America, one nation under God, being sent to an inhabited alien planet without any religious mandate."

"Sir, we don't have time to properly train a religious person for this mission. It's been eight months and we're about to move."

"Then find a way to make it happen."

"With our current resources?"

"Sure."

Travis looked at Mabel. "We can crash-course one of ours."

"Give him a prayer book," Mabel said, "and some holy water."

"And one of those swinging incense things," Chilblain said.

"And I know just which one of our guys, Mabel."

"Yeah, Travis?"

"Yeah."

"Methodist, remember," Chilblain said, looking back and forth between the twins, who seemed unable to take their eyes off each other.

xiv.

An hour after dawn, the access hatch of the *Jungles of Mars* sub-orbital transporter opened to the mild humming of its 18-volt generator. The walking ramp rolled out and the stabilizer spikes stuck in the ground.

A hundred feet away, Francine – or, Luhk -- wearing a bison-skin tube-top, leaned against a sandstone boulder adorned with the primitive drawings of tribesmen chasing a herd of wooly mountain goats. She held back a fierce yawn. Squatting behind her in the dusty grime, balancing on spears, a band of Uhluk hunters wearing glyptodon-shell head coverings and prosthetic upper-dentures quietly chastised themselves. No one had showered for four days – per the production proviso – and people were starting to itch like gibbons.

The plan: Go with the flow. Anticipate the improvisation. If the astronauts, played by Nick Boon, Ryan Konner and Alfie Leroux, decided to exit the transporter, the natives were supposed to flog themselves with pickleweed bladders and enact the often-rehearsed welcoming sequence. If nothing happened, they would get the signal from Jeffries – wherever he was – and probably break for lunch. But everyone was like, *come on*. After four stolid days rehearsing this scene, the tribe was positively begging for something to happen, especially Francine, playing the tribe's emissary.

She closed her eyes and tried to remember back to their endurance class, when these miserable, unshaven people actually looked normal, in spandex and cross-trainers with sweat streaks down their backs, complimenting each other's calves. But alas, each day it got harder to see them as anything but New World hunter-gatherers, roving in a small, semi-organized band through a pitiless wasteland that would one day be southern Nevada.

Meanwhile her Male Posessor, Roanoke – or, Beyzore – drew Ichthus fish in the dirt with his flint borer and Hunstiber, the Holy Man, waddled behind her, balancing on his Spirit Staff.

"I don't think we should be doing it this way," he said. "It's cowardly."

"Cavemen are not cowards!" Roanoke said, pumping his flint borer.

"We're not cavemen," Hunstiber said. "We're free-range hunters. You've been sleeping in the lectures."

"We all sleep in the lectures."

Hunstiber chanted under his breath.

"Shoo, Hunstiber!" Francine swatted him. "I don't like you hanging around my ass. Now everybody pipe down or we'll have to keep doing this again and again."

She, too, had concerns about this approach – specifically whether cavemen, or hunters, or whatever they were, would dare come this close to what her prop brief described as a 3000 kilogram, pressure resistant, sub-orbital lander with four Gimbal-mounted engines and a roving, high-gain antenna; do anything, really, other than cower behind the pole-and-thatch huts. She even voiced these concerns in the workshops. But Jeffries, as usual, disagreed.

"Pleistocene hunter-gatherers are bursting with curiosity, people," he had explained. "Though concerned with their own survival, they are discovering new innovations every day. Confronted with such a mind-blowing advancement in technology, they might see the visitors, you know, as a source of knowledge or spiritual transcendence. Or maybe they have some spare elk jerky. Go with your gut."

Of course, there was a reason they had to corral the aliens. The tribe's main objective – made explicit in the production proviso with ten, large, black exclamation points and a smiley face – was to contain the spacemen, at all costs, in the sparse crater, away from the Cave, away from the surface road, which "would allow them to wander and create mischief."

Francine edged around the boulder for a protected view of the transporter.

Four days of rolling dust winds had coated the solar reflectors, gathered clumps of creosote bush around the thruster fuel tanks and made the high-gain antenna twist like a weather vane on a barn. Francine could see, deep inside the access hatch, the rainbow-colored computer console. The mere sight of a passing shadow across those bright flecks, or the sound of someone lurking inside, would give the tribe a desperately needed sense of momentum. Instead, Francine braced herself for the swooping turkey vultures that had started hulking along the service ramp and squawking into the dark access hatch, egged on by the pompous sage grouses that flew down from the mountains to plume about the transporter and shit all over the exhaust vents.

Dawn passed. The sun shrunk to size, losing its ripe glow. A gray breeze swept down the veins of the crater and everyone braced for whirling heaps of dust and sagebrush. Thick green crickets ricocheted off the boulder, some latching to the camouflage tarp, and the chiggers itched on everyone's thighs.

Francine was resting her gaze upon the hypnotic contours of the Jarlsburg Butte, when she noticed a flash of light atop the rounded dome.

Jeffries' Afro – tweaked by his visor – peeked over the edge, and his round glasses glowed in the waning sun. He raised his bullhorn, which usually meant they were going to cut, break and rethink the scene; but just as he did, a guy in an orange jumpsuit and tiger-patterned helmet appeared in the access hatch.

Francine ducked behind the boulder and made a wide circle with her arms, tapped her knee and cocked her neck, which meant *get ready*. Hunstiber steadied the sandstone medallion on his spirit staff, while the others mussed their hair, rubbed dirt in their teeth and tightened their spear grips.

With a deliberate, ceremonial pace the spaceman ambled down the ramp.

Another appeared behind him with a briefcase; then a third, and they all stood staring in different directions.

Francine kept an eye on Jeffries, who leaned over the dome with binoculars. Doniphan, at his side, feebly raised a light meter.

The second spaceman removed an old TV antenna from the briefcase and made a sweep of the ground.

Francine got in her stance.

Jeffries, glued to his binoculars, raised his thumb.

The spacemen's pitch-black visors stared blankly ahead; the wind ceased, and everyone became seeped in the stillness.

This quiet moment was broken by a loud, shattering *pop!* over by the giant rock. Jeffries and Doniphan leaned over the edge to look down at the glorious, shattered mess of broken binocular pieces.

While the spacemen observed the scattered binocular pieces -- the middle one aiming his TV antenna at the debris – Francine stayed ready.

Jeffries smacked his forehead, which to her seemed like a good cue to get things going. She leaped out into the clearing. The spacemen turned, their moon boots pivoting gawkily.

Francine pounded her chest. She said, "Ooluk Yayooluk," and tore off her bison-skin top to reveal a poly-cotton T-shirt that read, *I'm What Willis Is Talkin' About.*

"Ooluk Yayooluk," chanted the tribe, skulking out and trembling, though mystically drawn to the spacemen, bent low, grunting and scratching, falling in place around Francine's feet.

Out of nowhere a turkey vulture swooped, landed on the middle spaceman's helmet and settled into a comfortable perch.

The bullhorn feedback popped.

"Nooooooo!" Jeffries now stood atop the giant rock, impervious, looking upom the scene like the Colossus of Rhodes, aiming his hunched torso at arbitrary points around the valley, and then at the dozen or so people below.

"Space people," he yelled. "D-Plus: You're not on the moon. Unless you have something crawling up your long johns, walk normal. Kay? Welcoming Tribe: C-Plus. It needs to be more... random. The way you come out. We're missing the *primal* nature of the exchange. Is everyone with me? Props?"

Bernice came out from behind the camouflage tarp, packing smokes.

"Is everybody with me?" Jeffries asked.

A grasshopper sprung into the clearing, and everyone stared at it.

"Ok," Jeffries said, pacing on the rock. "Does everyone remember *The Sound of Music*?"

Francine looked back at the tribe, all of them staring feverishly at the grasshopper.

She yelled to Jeffries, "What?"

"Does everyone remember that scene in *Sound of Music* where Christopher Plummer and Eleanor Parker and Richard Haydn are coming back from Vienna and they see all those kids in the trees wearing the green outfits Julie Andrews made from the old curtains in her room?"

Bernice hollered, "You asking Props?"

"Do you remember that scene, Donnie?"

Doniphan grabbed the bullhorn. "No. Please call me Doniphan."

Jeffries grabbed it back. "Well, that's what I'm talking about!"

He pulled out a snub-nosed pistol and shot a bending flare over the valley.

The actors grabbed waters and kicked back on the wicker mats, while a team of production assistants arranged sunscreens and doused people with mist sprayers. At the transporter, set techs started oiling the ramp belts, raked out the tumbleweeds and scrubbed the bird shit off the exhaust vents.

Francine, leaning on her elbows and licking the mist off her lips, hummed a song from The Cult's album *Love;* a song called "Love," while the cirrus clouds rolled above her as if on a conveyor.

XV.

Seen through the observation window in Goddard's Incubator Room, three fiberglass casks holding Ashby, Clark and Tongue lay in a row, connected to vital-sign monitors.

Goddard's resident psychiatrist, Dr. Emil Dunn, checked oxygen levels on the panel. "They look stable for transport, Drs. Mountjoy. But I strongly object to you going any further with this project. How much time deprivation have they experienced?"

"A lot," Mabel said. "They think it's a year from now."

"How did you do that exactly?"

"Sleeping pills, clock malfunctions, incubation simulation."

"Now they're on a Propofol drip while you transport them to Shacklett Air Force Base?"

"Correct."

"And you have absolutely no intention of taking them into space?"

"None."

"What happens when they wake up?"

The twins looked at each other and Dr. Dunn had the odd feeling they were about to kiss. He turned back to the panel and checked the vitals. Ashby's line ran calm, measured. Clark's showed occasional surges. Tongue's, though steady, had a wobbly twitch.

An invisible door opened in the wall and three Hazmat

techs wheeled out the casks.

"What if they realize what's going on?"

"They won't," Mabel said.

"How can you be so sure?"

"They'll believe what we tell them."

•••

Standing on a hangar loading dock, the Mountjoy Twins and Dr. Dunn watched a welding crew work on the VITRIOL passenger module, which was housed in the bed of a wide-load rig. Mounted spotlights illuminated the access hatch – a room with several lockers and equipment drawers and benches -- and a succession of detached modules: a command chamber, accommodation chamber and recreation chamber.

At the far end, Sharise Vanderslice climbed down the cockpit ladder. After checking the emergency cabinets and supply drawers, she flipped the climate console switches and pulled herself through the narrow passage.

"Ready as she'll ever be," she said, nodding hello to Dr. Dunn. "Most of what you see, Emil, is legit hardware: refrigeration chambers, re-hydratable storage, protein thermostabilizers, waste collection facilities -- top of the line. For safety, the nitrogen tanks are filled with salt water – they won't touch those anyway. And, of course, the fusion reactor is an electric decoy. It'll make an impressive noise and that's about it. No way in hell they would open any of it to check. Besides, the VITRIOL is a largely self-sufficient craft, requiring little maintenance, if any, of which the crew is aware. If they shut themselves up in here for any reason, they have plenty of supplies. We'll do a wireless hook-up from Shacklett's communications outpost to keep in touch through a video feed facilitated by a phony Decentralized

Observant Response Computer which talks and plays chess and stuff."

"Unbelievable," Dunn said.

They all moved aside as the Hazmat techs wheeled the incubator casks into the rig.

"Careful along that foyer," Sharise said. "Barely touch those fecal collectors and they pop right out."

"What is this experiment going to reveal exactly?" Dunn asked.

"Well, we need to know," Travis said, "how astronauts would react to such a situation."

Dunn laughed. "I can tell you that right now."

"Wait!" Travis pointed.

Dunn stepped back, startled.

"It's just the beginning," Mabel said. "Don't spoil it."

xvi.

Enoch Jeffries was basking in the top bunk, having his best sleep in weeks, when he awoke to a pounding noise. He leaned over the edge: Doniphan was smothered in bedclothes, crossways on the mattress, his arm dangling over the linoleum. Jeffries climbed down, stepped into his slippers and opened the door to find the hallway busy with lines of tall, fit military people carrying boxes to the defunct War Command Center.

Bare-chested Roanoke Sonoma, clutching a towel around his waist and his mammoth tusk totem, stood in the doorway of his room across the hall. "Get a load of these goobers."

Jeffries blinked at the stone-faced crew cuts marching up and down the hall. He stopped one. "At ease, brother."

The soldier stopped, staring ahead.

Jeffries, coming up to about the man's holster, tapped on the box. "Whatcha got in here?"

"Classified."

"Cover him, Roanoke," he said, grabbing the box.

Roanoke, not sure what to do, held up his mammoth tusk totem.

Jeffries tore open the box to find it filled with coiled wires and circuit boxes. "What is this garbage?"

"Looks like hubs and routers."

"Hubs n' who? Boy, you smell like skunk again."

Roanoke shrugged.

Jeffries weaved through the marching soldiers to find the military command center packed with teems of prematurely aged men in Oxford shirts and Dockers. The overhead screens ran with white numbers, the rotary phones clanged, the Plexiglass partition maps spun radar lines and against the far wall the Buick-size computer rumbled like a clothes dryer.

At the panel a woman in a blue jumpsuit was directing a group of programmers.

Jeffries wormed through the crowd and tapped her on the shoulder. "Lady, is this you?"

Sharise Vanderslice turned. "Is this me?" she said. "Meaning…?"

"This!" Jeffries waved around the room.

A techie swiveled around between them and asked, "COBOL II for this one, Dr. Vanderslice?"

"Nah," she replied. "Serve up some Easytrieve."

"Daddy," Jeffries said, "make the bad lady go away."

"See that big ole bear?" Sharise pointed at the computer. "That's an old-school MVS/DB2 mainframe. At one time, it could launch and sustain a large-scale military operation for six months, mapping every air, sea or ground movement on the planet. Of course it's been snoozing almost twenty years."

"Lady, I don't care of it snoozed through the last ten *Andy Williams' Christmas* specials. This is my happy place, and today is our first day of principal photography. We don't need you people in here gettin' all Doogie Houser and shit."

A programmer handed her a printout. "It's a lot of code, Doctor."

"By-pass it with C++. Call when you get stuck."

"Cool as hell," Doniphan said, standing in the doorway

wearing pinstripe boxers and a wife-beater, with Roanoke and Michelle peeking over his shoulder.

"I'm gonna *cool-as-hell* your ass." Jeffries snapped his fingers. "Everybody in Make-Up ASAP. Warm up the cameras. Call catering and have it done continental style. Tell the animal team to get the tigers, elephants and tortoises ready; and while you're at it, ask these jack-boot goobers if we can get a sniper to pick off the vultures."

Doniphan stood motionless, staring above Jeffries' head.

"Come on boy, you want a Threat Display?" Jeffries said, giving him the bird.

"My name is Doniphan," he replied in monotone, pointing up at the video panels.

The director turned and looked up.

•••

Hopping into the lounge, Jeffries pulled on his tennis shoes. Doniphan followed, snapping his shirt buttons. They ran through the reception area, knocking over card tables, bumping into naugahyde love seats, through the steel door, up the spiral staircase and curling around the cement pillar with the flickering safety lights. They bolted into the clearing. They could hear the sounds of a commotion, but couldn't see a thing through the dense clouds of dust.

The clouds heaved into a funnel as an H-21 Shawnee – a banana-shaped tandem-rotor helicopter – descended over the *Jungles of Mars* transporter. A rope dangled from the hatch. A man in black fatigues dropped onto the roof. After fastening hooks to the crane latches and slipping a hammock-like cradle beneath the undercarriage, he scaled back into the Shawnee and slammed the hatch. Two beats later, Jeffries watched as his beloved twenty-foot hunk of aluminum, fiberglass and old jet-ski parts drifted off like a battering ram and disappeared over the crater rim. Immediately, a team of soldiers surrounded the spot where the transporter had rested and torched it with flame-throwers.

The dust unfurled. The entire valley swarmed with HUMMERS, Bobcats and green-covered transport trucks, while a small army of special operations soldiers in black vests dismantled the entire set. Over by the barrow, one team hurled funeral pyre logs into the back of a truck, while another extracted the ceremonial arrows from the Tribal Chief's burial mound and flattened the barrow and beehive hovels with pitchforks and a gigantic tiller. An enormous truck with a scooper waited in the wings. On the far cliffs, six repellers flew down the edge and bounced gracefully on the footholds like champion skiers, stopping halfway down to drill holes into the rock. Back on the ground, near the surface incline, a rough terrain crane rumbled to the thatched banquet hall, lowered its mouth and clamped, making a sharp splintering sound, and dragged it up the incline.

The sage grouses and vultures circled the valley, watching all their usual perches disappear. Beyond the flattened barrow, the yaks had wandered out of their pen and were screaming at the soldiers. And in the sporadic moments of quiet, they could hear the wooly mammoths moan in the distance above.

Suddenly in the clearing, twenty feet from Jeffries and Doniphan, a pillar of air blasted the ground. They dropped and covered their heads as a Harrier Jump Jet, its nozzles blowing red exhaust, landed gently. The screaming engines stopped, the canopy opened and two people in flight gear descended the hatch ladder. Once on ground they paced backwards, thumbs high, and the plane rose in another fury of fire and air, splitting through the haze and forming a hole in the clouds.

They jogged toward the giant rock, hoisted the director and his assistant and they all hurried into the Cave, down the spiral staircase and into the reception area.

The helmets came off.

"No time to lose," Travis Mountjoy said, helping his sister with her hair twisty. "All-hands in the conference room!"

<u>Chief Lark Moon Triumphant at Keksoon-Dox</u>,
c. 1897
Robert C. Crimsondale, 1864-1923
Oil on Canvas
A Gift of the Betty-Ann Gilmore Collection

Painted during Crimsondale's sojourn in the American west among the Kiowah, Chief Lark Moon Triuphant at Keksoon-Dox, the first of his non-landscape paintings, showed the earliest example of his classical approach to the human form. The scene depicts a moment in the lore of the Meemaw Tribe, in which a Chief Lark Moon – grandson of Chief Meemaw – brings a horde of two-hundred Apache women, abducted in a raid, to Keksoon-Dox Camp near the Lampo-Po River valley in what is now western Nevada.

-- From <u>The Renwick Gallery Catalogue of the Permanent Collection</u>, Washington, D.C., 1994

xvii.

Francine had slept through the whole commotion. Apparently, a bunch of authority figures had infiltrated the Cave and now, without even a sip of coffee, they had all gotten corralled into the conference room to wait for some kind of *mission critical* announcement from Travis and Mabel, who had started to look eerily like Jennifer Jason-Leigh and Brigit Fonda, respectively, from *Single White Female*.

All the actors were there, plus a red-haired woman on a laptop and several armed soldiers leaning against the wall.

Jeffries sat at the head, clearly agitated and coated in dirt.

"Ladies and Gentlemen, welcome to *Operation EMU*," Travis said. "Mabel and I want to begin by expressing our sincere appreciation for the ingenuity and dedication you've put into the sets, props and rehearsals. As dramatic professionals, you should be very proud. I will now explain to you (a) the real reason you are all here and (b) why we have removed your camera crew, much of your intriguing set pieces and some of the animals."

Mabel said, "PowerPoint ready, Sharise?"

"Darn thing froze up."

"I apologize," Travis said. "We had a detailed presentation explaining our mission statement, but we may have to wing it."

"Basically," Mabel said, "we want to remind you that when you signed on – each and every one of you --" Mabel looked pointedly at Jeffries, "… you did so expressly to perform community service to offset felonies committed in violation of the U.S. Code. I am therefore *ordering* you to go with the flow."

"Now, who here believes in UFOs?" Travis asked.

A few hands rose.

"Radical. My sister and I run a government program called Clandestine Human/Extra-Terrestrial Operations, or, CHETO. We are responsible for defining the Standards of Operation with regard to how our interplanetary emissaries – or, astronauts – should act and interact with extra-terrestrials should they ever come in contact with one."

John LaZar mumbled something inaudible.

"What was that, sir?" Mabel asked.

"I just said extra-terrestrial etiquette."

"Exactly," Mabel said. "Big fan, by the way, Mr. LaZar. Now, at the inception of this program in 1949 our agency's sole responsibility was to provide the government with a myriad of scenarios in which our planet is visited by *advanced* extra-terrestrials who wish to (a) assist in our evolution with offerings of technological innovations, (b) admonish us for our self-destructive warmongering or (c) eat us. This was back when my grandfather ran the program."

"Since then," Travis said, "our fastidious studies, exploratory rovers and radio antennae have led us to the unfortunate conclusion that there are actually no *advanced* aliens anywhere nearby at this moment. On record, the only extra-terrestrial life we've found is a fungus on Mercury that grows overnight and gets incinerated as soon as the sun rises. That's classified, by the way." Travis pointed around the table. "You have all been cleared for this briefing and will be expected to maintain the confidentiality of what you hear."

"Now here's the interesting part," Mabel said. "We *have* discovered, beyond our solar system, parallel galaxies with planets similar to Earth. These planets have high H_2O percentages, minimal radiation and are optimally distant from the solar fulcrum, but none have reached our stage of development. Their life forms, if any, are behind us by anywhere from 8,000 to 20,000 years. NASA has estimated that in maybe thirty years, with adequate funding, we can transport a manned aircraft to these galaxies, which means CHETO is now responsible for preparing our astronauts; namely, to study how they react to a situation in which they land on an Earth-like planet populated by an underdeveloped, under-socialized version of themselves."

Sharise said, "PowerPoint!"

The lights dimmed. The projector beamed.

OPERATION E.M.U.
Experimental Mitigated Universe

"Thank you, Sharise," Travis said. "And now, actors, you may be wondering, 'How can I help the CHETO mission?'"

Travis clicked the remote.

MISSION
To Train Astronauts
For Extra-Terrestrial Encounters
In the U Majoris Galaxy
-- TOP SECRET --

"Covered that, sorry." Travis clicked the next slide.

OBJECTIVE
Study the Reactions & Interactions
Of Astronaut Subjects
In Said Prehistoric Environment
-- TOP SECRET --

"Using your costumes, props and new skills, you will *become* a late-Pleistocene, early-Holocene community here in the Stribling Valley."

METHOD
Conceive, Produce & Implement
A Simulated Prehistoric Environment
-- TOP SECRET --

"There will be no cameras, no cuts, no alternate takes and no breaks. You will stay in costume, stay in character and convince the astronauts -- to the best of your abilities -- that they have landed on an alien planet."

"And what happens if we don't?"

Mabel shined a penlight. "Who said that?"

Francine raised her hand.

"If you leave the set, if you disrupt the experiment, if you slip out of character even in the slightest, your governmental contract will be nullified. You'll immediately face a military tribunal at Shacklett Air Force base, be sentenced and shipped off to Guantanamo Bay."

Travis aimed the remote. "Now, here are some bullet points."

"Hold on a second." Hunstiber flipped on the lights. "This is absolute madness." Above the door the air vent came on, blowing his comb-over straight up like a sail. "Do you really think professional U.S. Government astronauts are going to think that we're actually aliens on another planet?"

Travis said, "I don't see why they wouldn't."

"I mean…" Michelle said. "Wanna explain how that's gonna work?"

"Mabel?" Travis offered the remote.

She pointed at Hunstiber, who hit the lights.

The screen showed photos of three men in sharp, blue military suits, each with cloudy blue backdrops and incredibly fake smiles. Francine tried to decide which of the *My Three Sons* they most resembled, but one of the photos in particular – the cute guy in the middle – made her pause, and she wasn't sure why.

"These are the men who will be visiting us in a short period of time." Mabel aimed her laser pointer. "This is the captain… this is his first mate… and this is the second mate. We've chosen them based on personality type, and we're curious to see how each reacts to this situation."

Roanoke raised his hand. "I don't get what makes them think they're on an alien planet."

"In missions involving this kind of distance, astronauts would be sedated for the majority of the flight to conserve resources. Over the last six months we've isolated them, deprived them of watches and calendars and gradually convinced them that they've been in training much longer than they actually have been. These men are currently under heavy sedation in a nearby hangar. Some time has passed; their fingernails and beards have grown. In a few days they will be placed in a ship we will assemble right outside in the valley. Eventually, their sedative drip will stop and they will be allowed to revive."

"Well," Roanoke asked, "won't they just look around and be able to tell this is Earth?"

"I doubt it," Travis said. "No one, except at the highest levels, knows this place even exists – this crater. And the high cliffs make it impossible to see the outer landscape."

"Planes?" Hunstiber said. "Flying out of Las Vegas?"

"This is government airspace a hundred miles in every direction," Travis said. "Nevertheless, all commercial and military traffic has been rerouted for the next two months."

Francine slapped the table. "The moon! What happens when they see the moon?"

"We're not really concerned." Mabel grabbed the Farmer's Almanac from her satchel. "Right now the lunar trajectory is low on the horizon. The moon will never cross the outer landscape. More importantly we're getting a swath of overcast skies, so we assume and hope there won't be much in the way of atmospheric landmarks. Meanwhile, you good people will be providing a delectable distraction on the ground."

"You're counting on overcast skies every day?"

"Let me ask you something," Travis said. "Say you get on a plane to Sandusky, Ohio. Before you take off the captain says, 'This plane is going to Sandusky.' When you land, do you ever really question that you're in Sandusky even though you've never been there before?"

"The point being," Mabel said. "We've trained these guys so thoroughly to trust in the mission that they *believe* they're landing on an alien planet. Nothing in the sky will change that."

On the projector, Mabel clicked through a series of photos detailing astronaut incubation, sedation, equipment and daily life. "These aren't that important," she said. "Any more questions?"

Travis switched on the light. Everyone groaned and stretched.

Jeffries, slumped in his chair, said, "So why is most of my set gone?"

"Want this one, Travis?"

"Sure, Sis. Mr. Jeffries, some of the set pieces were wrong for the period. In this part of Nevada -- 8,000 years ago – nobody got buried in barrows. That's more of a Druid thing. And the circle of arrows planted in the dirt didn't happen until the sixteenth century, and mainly the eastern tribes and stuff. Your thatched village was a tad too advanced, so we pulled some of it down. There are still enough huts to go around, but no banquet hall. This isn't *Beowulf.* People didn't have the engineering know-how to bend sticks that high. And the mammoths, I don't know... Maybe they wandered here after the last Ice Age? I'm still on the fence."

"It adds color, Goddamnit! These astronauts don't care about the accuracy of barrows and arrows and shit!"

"Mr. Jeffries." Mabel gave him a little shoulder rub. "You have to leave *some* technological achievements for the astronauts to teach them."

Nick Boon raised his hand. "Ryan, Alfonse and I have been playing the astronauts so far in rehearsals. What are we supposed to do now?"

Travis tapped his chin. "You can help operate the giant

robotic sloth."

The Props lady peeked in the room. "Who the hell paged me?"

"Ah, Bernice," Travis said. "Thank you for coming. Before we remove the costume trailer from the valley would you bring everyone's costume inside, leave every tool and implement – minus the blanket-weaving loom, which is about 5,000 years too advanced – out by the thatch village?"

"I guess," she said, packing smokes in her hand as she wandered off.

"Alright, people. More questions will come later I'm sure. Let's get our costumes on. It's time you got used to them – you'll be wearing those permanently the next few weeks."

Everyone had begun to file out when Travis yelled, "Hit the lights! I have one more slide to show you." He clicked the remote.

YOU CAN DO IT!
YOU CAN DO IT!
YOU CAN DO IT!
-- TOP SECRET --

Miggy Finch: Next caller is Rick from Santa Rosa, California. You're on the air.

Rick: Hello, Miggy. Hello, Professor Stacey. Thanks for taking my call. First, Professor Stacey, I want to say how much my reading group enjoyed your book – your latest one – on the theory of the Puerto Rican Chupacabra as a--

Miggy: We got 30 seconds before the break, Rick. What's your question?

Rick: Professor Stacey, I would like to know... I would like to ask whatever happened to... See, I heard you speak at the World Fantasy Convention in Sacramento-

William T. Stacey: Thanks for attending, Rick!

Rick: Yes, Sir. So, I was wondering about your book on Shrouded Rock and what's going on with it?

William: Ah. Frankly, Rick, it's been one disappointment after another.

Rick: Sorry to hear that.

William: Without a doubt... Miggy, do most of your listeners know about Shrouded Rock?

Miggy: Best explain, Bill.

William: Shrouded Rock is the largest, natural freestanding boulder in the world, but no one has ever photographed it or rendered it artistically, due to a long-standing dispute between the U.S. Government and Native American tribes that has made it virtually inaccessible, not to mention a boatload of innuendo fed by UFO theorists who think it's an intergalactic meeting place, environmental protestors who think it's a designated nuclear waste dump and New Age spiritualists who believe it has a magnetic-vortex inner chamber with acoustic healing effects. It's called Shrouded Rock because the Indians once covered it in an enormous tarp of sewn blankets. But, that's a whole 'nother story.

Miggy: Where is it supposed to be, Professor?

Rick: Um, the Right to Know Map of the Universe says Wyoming.

William: We just don't know. The Indians have an oral history, but the exact location is unknown and the government sure isn't going to say. But, the cognoscenti say it's situated deep inside a military base somewhere out west.

--Transcript from July 7, 1997, Radio Free Planet: With Miggy Finch.

xviii.

Nimrod Ashby dreamed he was walking on the ocean floor. He was wearing an old-fashioned diver's suit, connected to an air tube that moved with the currents. He ambled past pulsating coral beds and giant man-eating clams while shadows moved just beyond his line of sight. He blinked and everything turned bright. He looked up through the glass faceplate of his incubation cask. A red sensor on the ceiling recognized his body motion. The rubber sealant peeled apart and the incubator cask opened to the side.

He unbuckled the safety straps. After extracting the IV needles and unhooking the catheter tube from the folds of his undergarment, he sat on the edge and squeezed at his numb thighs, trying to calm the tremors.

Ashby stumbled to the washroom, stuffed his undergarment in the waste vacuum, put on a pair of briefs and a blue jumpsuit, and turned on the faucet. It sputtered with air before a thin, cold stream fell into his hands. He splashed his face and tugged at his dripping beard, looking in the small square of a mirror at his bloodshot eyes, deeply into his dilated pupils.

After drying his face with a paper towel, he staggered to the urine collection apparatus and leaned his head against the wall while he took a real piss for the first time in probably eight months.

Down the short passage between the services core and hibernation room, Ashby climbed the ladder into the command module, a circular rotunda that housed the cockpit and data center.

When he got to the top he heard "Hello, Nimrod" from a monitor above the control panel. "This is your Decentralized Observant Response Computer. It is Monday, June 16th, Year 20--. Planetary capture and landing successful."

"Thank you, DORC," Ashby said, sitting at the control panel. "Damage sustained?"

"Negative."

"Reactor coolant engaged?"

"Affirmative."

"How about the payload tanks?"

"Tight."

"Stop Propofol on Colonel Clark and Captain Tongue, please."

"Stop Propofol initiated, Nimrod."

Ashby flipped a switch on the panel, activating the external dosemeter to check surface radiation levels. "You can go ahead and call me Colonel Ashby."

"Gladly," DORC said. "Would you like to play chess, Colonel?"

Ashby reached for the Visor Block release button, which raised the cockpit's titanium-plated window protectors, but decided to wait. He wasn't ready to see the planet's surface yet. It was too much to take in at once.

"Maybe later," he said. "First, I need outside temperature, gravity, pressure and radiation stats."

Ashby climbed back down to the latrine and grabbed an aspirin from the first-aid packets, plus a laxative and a multivitamin he washed down with Tang. On his way back through the hibernation room, he found Erasmus J.T. Clark sitting up, staring blearily ahead, touching his beard.

"Can I help?" Ashby asked.

"I'm good," Clark said, trying to stand, but still hooked to his vital connectors. "Are we… you know, here?"

"Yes."

"Okay." Clark inhaled sharply. His bony shoulders trembled. He looked around the chamber. "I feel like I'm going to be sick."

Ashby unhooked his catheter and IV, and led him to the latrine.

When Ashby returned to the incubator room, he found Captain Tongue stretched out in the opened cask, his hands folded neatly over his stomach.

"Captain Tongue, can you hear me?"

"Mmm."

"We've landed."

Tongue opened his eyes and said, "Shit."

From the latrine, they heard the tinny sound of Colonel Clark dry heaving.

•••

"Temperature is 22ºC, oxygen pressure 1000 millibars, Gravity 1, humidity 35% with overcast skies," DORC said. "Radiation level is 0.12 rem per year."

"Sounds like home." Ashby unlocked the safe under his command panel and removed the mission files.

"That is correct, Colonel Ashby. The climate is very similar to that of Earth. Radiation levels are slightly higher, though not prohibitively."

Ashby took a deep breath and let it out. He pushed the Visor button. The shield rose slowly around the cockpit. Soon the 360-degree window revealed the arid surface of 47 U Maj D.

Clark scaled the ladder and went directly to the window. "It's beautiful."

"Hello, Colonel Clark," DORC said.

"Hello, DORC. How was the flight?"

"Fine, Colonel Clark. Our mass driver navigated several treacherous asteroid fields and we encountered the Trifid Nebula, both of which are saved on the video server. Besides that and our black hole entry, I would say an uneventful passage."

Clark, still looking slightly crazed, stumbled to his co-pilot's panel. "I wish I could have seen that black hole," he said. "Any video of that?"

"A/V systems encountered interference upon entry, leaving no video for the duration of the mission, including orbit insertion and landing. Colonel Clark, could I interest you in a game of chess?"

"Ah… you know, DORC, I think I'll take a rain check."

"Cribbage?"

"Need an ETA on A/V repairs, DORC," Ashby said.

"A/V completely functional since yesterday, Colonel Ashby. A Mission Control communication arrived four days ago. Should I play it now?"

"Yes, please."

A female voice crackled through the intercom.

Crew of the VITRIOL: If you are listening to this feed, you have arrived on 47 U Maj D in 47 Ursae Majoris after a successful remote landing managed by Skylab X. Congratulations. Mission guidelines can be found in the safe. We recommend several days

of monitoring habitability stats before leaving the transporter.
Contact Skylab X for a video conference. Over, out.

"DORC, please arrange video conference with Skylab."

"Right away, Colonel Ashby... Good morning, Captain Tongue."

"Holy shit," T.W. Tongue said, leaning on the ladder railing, staring out the back window at the cliff's edge. "What do we know?"

"Stats are normal," Ashby said. "Conceivably, we could go out in light explorer gear. Skylab says wait two days to be sure."

"The sky worries me."

"It's just a weather system. Simple accumulation. It should blow away soon."

"And then what?"

Ashby swiveled around. "T.W., I know it's a shock to finally be here. I suggest you stay busy and help us troubleshoot the maintenance of the Ramscoop funnel."

Ashby checked printouts of the ship's propellant reserves -- to monitor conservation for eventual liftoff – and displayed a video triptych of the surrounding desert. "DORC, where are we located exactly?"

"We have landed in a remote desert region, Colonel, a thousand miles from the nearest ocean. Our approximate location is latitude 45, longitude 125. We are 20,000 feet above sea level."

"Is that a mountain ahead of us?"

"We appear to be in a natural crater, Colonel."

"That's unfortunate. If our rover can't scale the valley cliffs, we'll have to climb out with the surveillance gear."

A static buzz came from the DORC screen. "VITRIOL

Crew: I've detected a small malfunction in the reactor propulsion coolant system."

"Can you fix it?" Ashby asked.

"Affirmative. I will need to switch to maintenance panel, making me unavailable for approximately… thirty minutes. Is that acceptable?"

"Affirmative. Whatever it takes."

Just as the screen went dark Captain Tongue said, "Wait! DORC? Shit. What about life signs? Anybody do an infrared survey? Fuck!" Tongue breathed from his shoulders. He went to his pilot's station and opened a cabinet. He removed a safety kit, a notepad and a folded garment. "What the fuck is this?" He unfolded what looked like a long black dress.

"Looks like a Roman Catholic cassock," Ashby said. "Note the collar. That's part of your missionary gear, I assume."

Tongue pulled out a rosary, a crucifix and a Book of Common Prayer with the initials *T.W.T.* embossed in gold. "I just want you guys to know right off the bat that I'm not putting this ridiculous thing on."

"Do your best, Captain."

Erasmus Clark, still at his panel, had begun to tremble. He quickly released the high-gain-antenna joystick and grabbed his armrests. Suddenly he shot up and ran for the ladder screaming, "Get me out of here!"

Ashby tackled Clark. They fell to the floor. Fearing a seizure Ashby grabbed a rock specimen brush from a utility satchel and inserted it between Clark's front teeth.

"Captain Tongue," he called out. "I'd appreciate your assistance here."

Tongue was gazing out the window. "Take a moment, friends," he said. "And get a load of that."

] 120 [

xix.

A few moments earlier, Sharise Vanderslice said, "Bingo," tapping the video screen that showed the astronauts sitting at their cockpit panels. "They'll probably rotate the command module to face the thatch village. If not, DORC should recommend it, citing radiation exposure as an excuse…Whew!" She leaned against the Plexi-glass radar map. "Great job everyone. Take five and then we'll prepare Skylab video conference feed."

The programmers broke from their workstations.

Sharise went to the soundproof room and tapped on the window. "Easy on the chess, Yuri."

Inside the studio a man with a peaked, bald head removed his headphones, muttering. He opened the door. "If I don't play soon I'm going to explode!"

"These guys may not be the type, you know. Pitch some online poker next time."

As Yuri disappeared Jeffries entered the command center. "How's life, Mary Hartman?"

"Eh." Sharise waved him into the War Room. "Never should have picked a treasonous chess champion to play the voice of DORC."

"I mean out there."

"Well, check out the monitors. Pretty exciting stuff. VITRIOL crew woke up about two hours ago."

"'Bout time, baby. Natives are restless."

"As they should be. God just landed in their backyard."

"God better hurry on up."

"Meaning?"

"Listen, honey. For four straight days, my tribe's been out in the flats, scraping flint and drinking goatskins filled with Dasani. Waiting."

"What do you want me to do about it?"

"Tell your turkeys to come outside and play."

"Not for a few days, I'm afraid. Protocol."

"You gotta nudge 'em a little."

"They'll think I'm endangering them."

Jeffries strolled around, swinging his bullhorn like the Little Tramp.

"Don't touch anything, Jeffries."

"You know what this reminds me of?"

"Hmm?"

"Remember *Straw Dogs*?"

"Peckinpah," she said, dreamily. "Always wanted to, but --"

"Anyway, remember that scene where Susan George is running upstairs to change shirts and out the window she sees T.P. McKenna, Peter Arne and Jim Norton laying shingles on the greenhouse roof, and they see her and she just stands there half-naked with that defiant look on her face?"

The emergency buzzer sounded.

"Rats," Sharise said. "Can you yell for Yuri?"

Jeffries' looked up at the monitor and said, "Well, shiver me timbers."

XX.

James McElroy – grimy and naked except for a yak hair tunic and leg wraps -- raised his spear and grunted, "Ooh-ooh-ooh." He nodded to his team – half a dozen identical figures -- and sprinted across the clearing, streaking trails of dust, while the others followed.

A hundred feet from the spacecraft they stopped abruptly and hurled the spears. McElroy's soared beautifully, dropped and bounced off the middle reactor with a tinny clank. The others too fell short, only getting as far as the lower boosters. But Roanoke's spear made a marvelous arch, seemingly headed over the funnel, but eventually dropped and smashed right through a cockpit window.

"Holy shit," he said, unable to move.

The hunters, dumbfounded, watched the orange shards wobble and fall like broken teeth, and soon the astronauts peeked out of the shattered hole.

McElroy said, "Ooh-ooh-ooh," and the others formed a semi-circle, chanting and pounding their chests until he whispered, "Let's get the fuck out of here," and they sprinted back to the village and immediately began pounding moss patches on sandstone flats.

xxi.

Francine was jointing the hindquarters of an elk when Roanoke came bounding into the wigwam like a house on fire.

She raised her hands, signing *what is it?*

He smacked his head so hard his upper-dentures popped loose.

She tapped her chin. *Are you in pain?*

He squatted in the corner.

She patted his shoulder -- *it's okay* -- and laid out bits of meat for their dinner before starting the jointing again, using a sharp flint to split the backbone, occasionally peeking through the trusses at the spaceship, trying with all her might to get worked up over something that looked like a ride at Six Flags. Eventually she'd have to join the other wives for Gift-Giving, and she wanted to be able to evoke some genuine fear.

The tarp flapped open. McElroy ducked inside. "Chief says go back for the spears."

"Right now?" Roanoke asked. "Aren't we supposed to be afraid?"

"Our spears are extensions of ourselves."

Francine gestured for them to shut-up and stay in character.

"Silence, woman!" McElroy said.

"Fuck you, dickhead," she replied.

He crouched and said, to the dirt, "we broke the spaceship."

"Do you think I give a shit? Look at all these spleens I have to empty before nightfall."

Roanoke pounded his chest. "Don't silence my woman, Nahlak."

"Uh, I'm the lead hunter."

"I know. I'm just saying… Beyzore is sensitive to stuff. He could attempt to overthrow you."

"Doubtful. I would slay you in combat."

Hunstiber opened the tarp with his Spirit Staff. "Gentlemen," he whispered. "I can hear you all the way to the salt lick."

"Hand gestures please," Francine hissed. "And take it outside."

Once alone, Francine – or, Luhk -- collapsed on her mat and resorted, again, to fantasizing about being with a hunter who treated her better.

Beyzore – Roanoke's character -- hadn't been hunting in days, staying near camp to poke the fire and gather basket twigs when Luhk already had plenty. Earlier that morning, when she returned from fetching mammoth dung for kindling, he stepped on a piece of sharp flint and angrily complained about her decorative sod grass arrangements. He sulked in the corner and rubbed his foot, eventually giving her the *sorry* hand signal, grinding his finger in his hand and marking a tear on his cheek. And so it had gone for days: fights started haphazardly and ended with weak resolves.

And this was the life she led, and this was her man, and at the end of the day she had little to show for it. Some of the other hunters returned from furlongs with nick-nacks for their women, like eagle feathers, dried wishbones and muskrat skulls. Beyzore had never brought her a thing. Once when he returned from a hunt and, in typical fashion, dropped a hide on the floor without even saying hello, she mentioned this fact and he signed, *are you never satisfied?* She couldn't understand what the big deal was: all he had to do was sneak into the Cave and fish something out of the Prop Box, for God's sake. Even an elk hoof would do the trick.

Some evenings she stayed awake listening to simulated sex in neighboring huts, sometimes reaching peaks of curious arousal, depending on the skill level of the actors. Francine's character, Luhk, was barren, and sexual intercourse with her Male Possessor had dropped off, as he realized that other women grew big bellies (actually, unbecoming stomach prostheses) as a result of this intercourse, while his woman did not. Not only was she unable to reproduce, she refused to prance around in blue paint like the other hunters' wives, preferring a thin, elk-skin shawl with some nice quill-feather trimming.

And that was the extent of their passion. Though some nights Roanoke would wake in a panic, clawing at her lambs' wool blanket, mounting her and managing some futile humps before collapsing in sleep. Just the night before, he woke her, his eyes glazed, madly waving his arms, and initiated a strange conversation with hand gestures.

Beyzore: *Your hair feels like spider webs across my face.*
Luhk: *I want to go back to sleep.*
Beyzore: *I am afraid of dying.*
Luhk: *Tomorrow.*
Beyzore: *No. Tonight. You hate me for being weak.*
Luhk: *We've gone over this before.*
Beyzore: *Your hair feels like spider webs across my face.*
Luhk: *Then get out. I'm tired.*

After this exchange, she rolled over. He grabbed her rump, pulled her up and dry-humped her while she swatted him with her nettle pillow, crying for help and finally succumbing into firm submissiveness until his bleak, climactic moan drifted off like a lost balloon.

Beyzore had an excuse for his behavior, as did everyone: the spaceship that landed several days ago had changed everything. While they awaited the retribution of this flaming metal eagle, this flying totem, no one could possibly engage in normal activities. Considering that the Uhluk still prayed every evening for the sun to rise again, and engaged in dozens of obsessive rituals to ensure a good rain and bountiful hunts, the mere fact that this powerful object had landed a few hundred yards away seemed to call everything into question. Was it their creator, who kept them satisfied with food and occasional merriment? Was it a harbinger of destruction? Was it going to eat them? Francine had chosen not to panic. The other women had been self-chastising in public, but Francine stayed away from that, which was okay. Her character had no children, an unhappy marriage, and every single one of her days slouched into the next. So the spaceship, or whatever it symbolized, might as well have landed on *her* for all she cared.

Yet, in spite of all this hopelessness, she managed to preserve the meat, keep the fire going, the wigwam insulation hanging, and found time to socialize every afternoon with the other wives while they boiled deer brains to make fabric softener.

Francine crawled out of the wigwam. From the far southwest, thunder rumbled. She stretched and yawned, remembering to keep a low center of gravity, and sashayed past the fire, where the hunters were huddling with John LaZar and Hunstiber. She made her way over to where Gail and a few others were milking yaks into carved sandstone basins. Francine sat on a nearby rock and watched bugs bounce off Gail's ratty wet hair and her dangling blue breasts.

Gail said, "Ayacha," the word for yak milk.

"Ayacha." Francine stroked the yak. "*What the fuck is going on?*"

Gail struggled with a complicated gesture, eventually giving up. "Window," she said, which they didn't have a gesture for.

From the fire came some light chanting. The hunters sprinted toward the spaceship, making the buzzards scatter. They stopped, stooped and fetched their spears, running back to the fire where Roanoke, John LaZar and Hunstiber were whooping and heckling supportively.

Roanoke, seeing the men bragging with their spears, suddenly realized he didn't have a spear, as his had gone through the cockpit window.

He stomped over to Francine and said "Hoono."

"Hoono?" she replied.

"Hoono!" He beat his chest.

Gail whispered, "I think he's asking you to make him a new spear."

Francine, leaning on her knees, looked up at Roanoke. He didn't waver. She grabbed a limb from the kindling pile and returned to the wigwam. Before opening the tent flap she turned around. Roanoke was sauntering around Gail, watching her milk the yak with a lascivious look.

McElroy – Gail's Male Possessor – noticed. He ran over and tackled Roanoke to the ground. Roanoke gained the edge and pinned McElroy's shoulders. He leaned close and hissed "Kalatra Ka!" – probably the worst thing he could have said, meaning he would feed his body to the mammoths and afterwards lay happily with his wife on a parchment. McElroy reached for a sandstone bowl just as John LaZar blew his goat horn and yelled "Uhluk! Ahtrah Mai!" – or, *Warning Uhluk Tribe!*

On the access ramp of the spaceship, two astronauts in full space gear were descending, one of them carrying Roanoke's spear.

"Another example of the inseparability of the material and spiritual in Native Americana can be found in the so-called 'medicine bundles' that encapsulated a tribe's successes in hunting, battle, crops or visionary dreams. The contents of such a bundle – often preserved in an animal-skin pouch and containing significant miscellany such as broken arrows, scalps and rare animal skulls – were used in regular, ritualistic ceremony and sustained a virtual universe for the tribe, the loss of which could result in disbandment. The most tragic of these occurrences on record involved Nevada's mythical Meemaw, a gratuitous clan whose medicine bundle had served largely in their bigamous marriage ceremonies and buffalo meat orgies."

--Karson C. Klugen, "Dawn of Spiritual America," from The Fort Lauderdale Journal of Christian Theory: Issue No. 345; April 1999

xxii.

As he stepped down the VITRIOL ramp, Erasmus Clark recalled what his grandfather once told him about seeing bobcats in the woods: *They're more afraid of you than you are of them*; but he could hardly keep a grip on the wooden spear as he and Ashby walked toward the natives' campsite, where the hairy figures by the bonfire angrily waved their weapons. He reached down to caress the thumb lock of his TASER Blade-Tech stun gun, and somehow felt better.

Halfway there, Ashby stopped. Clark continued ahead and laid the spear lengthwise on the ground. He returned to Ashby.

The natives quietly pondered this gesture.

Through the tint of his Gemini helmet visor Clark observed their hand signals, some of which made sense; like the chest poundings (*pride? self?*) and the pinky and thumb out like wings (*the VITRIOL craft? flying*). He hoped at some point to learn these signals and to converse with these people. Though the mission guidelines stipulated that the VITRIOL crew should affect the natives as little as possible, leaving intact their natural growth and development, Clark wanted to engage in some kind of communication. And besides, the longer he thought about it, the more useless the mission guidelines seemed. He noticed the confusion in the natives' gestures, their awe and fear of the VITRIOL craft, and realized that no pre-planned approach could reverse the enormity of what was happening to these people.

The natives scattered into their dwellings; a few, Clark noticed, ducked under the large rock near the campsite.

Through the cockpit receiver Clark heard Captain Tongue say, "That's all, folks."

Ashby said, "Let's try this again tomorrow. Maybe go a little closer."

One of the natives yelled, "Alakya! Alakya!"

Four females scurried out with baskets. They formed a line fifty yards away, facing the astronauts.

"Okay," Ashby said. "Let's stay put."

The females, flanked by two tough-looking males, began to approach in a perfect line.

"Don't make a move unless I say so, Colonel Clark."

"Or unless threatened," Tongue said.

"Wait for my signal."

As the natives approached Clark wondered how strange and ridiculous they must appear to them, wearing full space gear, their heads covered in big orange helmets. They should have come out in standard jumpsuits, so the natives could see that they were practically the same species. Though 47 U Maj D's atmospheric readings were conducive to human life, with plenty of oxygen and almost minimal radiation, Ashby insisted they wear full-protective gear on the surface for a few days. As the natives drew closer, in their agonizingly slow march, Clark noticed that three of the females wore fur vests, with dusty blue grime covering their shoulders and arms, but that the fourth female wore a different garment that covered her shoulders and torso completely. He pointed this out to Ashby and Tongue. "She must be important. Older. Maybe a queen."

"Or a leper," Tongue said.

"Treat everyone equally," Ashby said, "unless they signal otherwise."

Ten feet away the group stopped. One of the males ran ahead and grabbed the returned spear. The females placed animal-skin mats on the ground and knelt on them. They held out egg-shaped baskets and bowed their heads. The males stood on either side, leaning on their spears.

Ashby said, "Nobody move." He took a step forward. Since the males didn't tense, he continued until he was within reach of the females.

The first one handed him a dead quail. She bowed. He bowed in reply and moved to the second, who laid a bouquet of dried leaves filled with buckeyes next to the quail; the third offered a large rodent's skull; and the fourth woman – the one wearing the tan covering – gave an impressive gift: a bird made of intricately folded palm leaves. Soon he had an odd collection of things spread out upon his insulated gloves. Ashby bowed and, without thinking, moved to the next person – one of the males – and held out his hands. Immediately Ashby knew he'd made a mistake. Instead of making a sudden move, however, he paused to observe the grimy man's long, tangled hair and his rough, sunburned face. Ashby felt a quiet terror, as if he were floating beside a shadowy creature in deep waters.

The native man seemed confused. He tucked the spear under his arm and searched his pockets, eventually pulling a carved object out of his waist pouch. After a blip of hesitation he placed it in Ashby's hands.

Though he faced a being that lagged behind him in developmental intelligence by more than 8,000 years Ashby could feel a complex emotion coming from him, and knew instantly that the man had parted with an object that had deep, sentimental value. Ashby bowed, and returned to Colonel Clark.

As the males steadily beat their spear butts, the females rose to standing. The male on the right chanted "Tooluk-Ta! Tooluk-Ta!" and immediately the females removed their vests, baring their dusty blue breasts; that is, except for the woman in the tan covering, the one who had offered the sophisticated palm bird, who now stared vacantly over the astronauts' helmets.

"Tooluk-Ta!" the rightward male repeated, flushed. But the woman stared straight ahead.

After an awkward pause the females, including the one in tan, launched into an interpretive dance using eagle feathers and finger-bone whistles and wild arm movements; and during this dance, which seemed to go on forever, Erasmus Clark couldn't take his eyes off the woman who had refused to remove her covering, transfixed by her sinuous movements and whisking hair.

As if in a trance Clark unhooked the pressure clamps on his Gemini helmet and peeled away the suction protectors.

Ashby said, "Colonel Clark, stop."

Clark dropped the suction protectors, with the sound of Ashby's voice saying, "Colonel Clark, I am ordering you to…." drifting away with the helmet. He tucked it under his arm and broke another mission rule -- *refrain from looking the natives directly in the eyes.*

When the woman saw Clark she stopped dancing. The native and the astronaut stared at each other for long uninterrupted seconds, each of them sharing in the realization that they were being perceived and considered and compared by the other; while the ceremonial dancers waved eagle feathers in the woman's face, trying to get her to continue with the performance. Clark felt his body's stiffness subside as he drifted into a reverie in which he fell into a prolonged sleep, waking with his head in this woman's lap, his hands reaching for her hair, nestled in a wood-smoked hovel in some far-flung corner of the universe.

xxiii.

In the Cave's conference room, Francine sat in a high-backed leather chair while Jeffries paced behind her.

"Baby, I know I should be surprised about all this happening," he said. "But somehow I ain't. We had a deal, no?"

"I don't understand why you're so mad."

"I'm mad, too," Doniphan said, nursing a Dasani.

Francine gave him the finger.

Jeffries sat on the table. "Now, why am I so mad about this?"

"Maybe because you have no idea what it's like out there. It sucks. I'm tired of delousing people and I can't get that buffalo spleen smell off my hands."

"Ever see *Loneliness of the Long-Distance Runner*?"

"Ugh."

"…that part near the end where Tom Courteney is running up the hill toward Michael Redgrave and the cheering crowd, and all of a sudden he stops before he reaches the finish line and just stands there while the rich kids sprint past him and win the cup?"

"That has nothing to do with this, Jeffries."

"Here's what I'm saying, baby: You're not 1950's English working-class penal system fodder thumbing your nose at the establishment, and I'm not the warder of a borstal packing my pipe on the green, and *he*'s not Topsey Jane in a wool skirt working at the library all her life."

"Wait," Doniphan said. "Topsey Jane?"

"The girlfriend."

"Sure about that?"

"Blonde hair. Pretty face. Sad. Like the girl in *On the Waterfront*. Jill St. John."

"Eehnk!" Doniphan made an X with his arms. "Jill St. John was the chick in *Diamonds Are Forever*."

"Shit," Jeffries said. "Then who was that dame?"

"Not Topsey Jane."

"Goddamnit, Doniphan!" He hurled his visor at the wall map of Cambodia. "I mean from *On the Waterfront*."

"Eva Marie Saint," Sharise Vanderslice said, standing in the doorway wearing a 14th Century Red Courtesan dress with gold embroidery.

"What the Jesus?"

"Listen, Jeffries," she said, straightening her jeweled belt, "I need your Uhluk Tribe to cool it with the spears."

"What happened to you, honey?"

"Historical costuming helps me de-stress."

Jeffries snapped his fingers at Doniphan. "Eva Marie Saint. Take my word for it, Donnie. Spitting image of Topsey Jane."

Doniphan propped his red Pumas on the table. "I still say she wasn't in *Loneliness of a Long-Distance Runner*."

Sharise cleared her throat loudly. "Keep the spears and slingshots on the down-low, fellas. VITRIOL may be a prototype craft, but it's my baby."

"Duly noted." Jeffries fetched his visor.

"And I'm worried about an altercation if my crew gets spooked." She curtseyed and ducked away.

Roanoke peeked in the doorway, clutching a bundle of elk hooves. "Beyzore needs you, Francine."

She sighed. "Make your own dinner."

"And hey," he said, turning to leave, "that little origami swan thing you gave the astronauts? Props didn't authorize it whatever it was."

"Yeah," Bernice said, peeking out behind Roanoke.

Francine rolled her eyes. She turned to Jeffries. "I used to go to a sushi bar in Pasadena where they made those for the kids."

Roanoke shook his head. "I can't work with this."

"But that's not how *Loneliness of the Long-Distance Runner* ends, people," Jeffries said, looking between his hands. "The last thing we see is this long table with a bunch of kids laboring, and Tom Courteney sitting there fixing a transistor radio and it's hard to tell whether he's miserable or satisfied or what, and then it goes dark."

Francine folded her arms. "So, you're going to give me more work, huh? Make me pestle wheat germ all night by the fire?"

"No. But I'm afraid I gotta make an example of you."

"Ok. Whatever. Fine."

"It makes sense," Doniphan said, tossing her an orange Now-And-Later. "These hunters wouldn't tolerate such behavior from a squaw."

"Don't eat that," Jeffries said. "Orange tongue."

She threw it at him. "I'm not going topless."

"Grrrrrrr!" Jeffries slapped his forehead. "Baby, I can't have you acting all insubordinate to the tribal code. Not only are you setting yourself apart from the other wives, you're making Beyzore look like the dick."

"I just can't."

"Why?"

"Because."

"Just give me one acceptable reason."

"Okay," Francine said. "You know the astronaut who took off his helmet?"

"Mr. Weird Guy, yeah. What about him?"

Francine clutched her shawl. "We went to high school together."

"What!" Jeffries yelped, biting his hand.

Doniphan leaned forward. "Francine, are you totally goddamned sure about that?"

"Yeah I'm totally goddamned sure, Doniphan. I asked him to the Sadie Hawkins dance."

XXIV.

"Congratulations, VITRIOL Crew," Sharise Vanderslice said, wearing a blue NASA jumpsuit, framed by the cockpit's video monitor. "You've made intergalactic history."

"Thanks, Professor," Ashby said. "I still can't believe it."

"DORC and Skylab X crunched the atmospheric numbers, so feel free to walk upon the surface without protective gear."

Clark said, "47 U Maj D's atmosphere is still overcast with cloud accumulation."

"Yeppers. You might not see the sky before departure. Where is Captain Tongue?"

Tongue stood on a chair at other end of the cockpit, ripping long pieces of duct tape off a roll between his knees, holding a plastic sheet over the broken window.

"What do you suggest for sealing that window, Professor?" Ashby asked.

"Errr… I'm still sore about that," Sharise said. "When the visors lower it'll be close to solid. But you're right to ask. DORC?"

"Yes, Professor?"

"Window sealant ideas?"

"There should be scrap metal patches for repairs in the hold, along with welding equipment."

"Solid enough for flight?"

"Affirmative," DORC said. "I can test to be sure."

"Great then," Sharise said, her feed turning static. "Nothing to worry about."

•••

Ashby leaned back in the pilot's chair and examined the object he'd received from the hunter, roughly the size of a banana and made of polished rock. It was an abstract depiction: two deer heads connected, without bodies, surging at opposite ends.

"DORC, what do you make of this object?"

"Could you hold it higher, Colonel?"

Captain Tongue said, ripping some tape with his teeth, "It's a weapon."

"It has a handle grip, Colonel Ashby," DORC said. "But no perforated, serrated or sharp edges."

"Hmm," Ashby said. "Therefore not a weapon."

"I would say it's a spiritual device. A totem, if you will."

Erasmus Clark arrived with three trays in one hand, the other holding a clear plastic bag filled with a soft brown substance. "Lunch," he called.

Tongue grabbed his tray, which had five compartments filled with flat, gelatinous foods. He sat at a small white table and unwrapped his sterile utensils.

"Boss?" Clark held out a tray.

Ashby stared at the ivory object. Considering the blunt tools available to these 47 U Maj D natives, the carving was fairly sophisticated. The sleekness of the animal heads, the power of the hind legs and the nobility of the faces gave them a distinguished, human appearance. Maybe the animals rendered in the carving had been ones the man had hunted, or maybe he'd seen them in a dream exactly as rendered -- two heads connected without a body -- and turned the vision into something he could show to people or carry on his travels. How could anyone know for sure? But it was obvious that the man who had made it must have done so with real affection.

Clark hoisted the heavy plastic bag over his plate and let a soft brown substance ooze from the corner cap.

"Squeeze me some more of that beanie-weenie?" Tongue said, holding out his tray. "You know, Colonel Ashby, I don't know what you're thinking but you can't give that thing back."

"Correct," Ashby said, leaving the carving on his console and joining the others at the table.

"You could give him something in exchange," Clark said, pushing his tray aside.

From the DORC panel they heard, "Are you done eating, Lt. Colonel Clark?"

Clark looked up. "Um… I think so."

"Chess?"

After some hesitation he said, "Let's do it."

Ashby, meanwhile, chewed slowly, staring at the dark space under the pilot's panel. Suddenly he dropped his fork and went to the window. Out by the bonfire the hunters had gathered with spears and skin satchels tied around their waists, while the man in the long-flowing animal skin held a staff over their heads. After what looked like a brief prayer the hunters wandered off behind the village to a long, mounting pathway on the edge of the cliffs that led out of the valley, leaving the females at work around the huts, arranging the moss patches and animal skins that had fallen off the dwellings. Ashby had not noticed any goodbyes.

"Check mate," DORC said.

"Hey, wait." Clark leaned close to the screen. "How did you

do that?"

"That's a simple *sui-mate*, Colonel Clark. An old Bobby Fischer stand-by."

"Whoa."

"Another game?"

"Do you have an Intermediate level?"

Ashby said, "DORC, I have an odd question," watching the hunters walk the incline to the surface. "What do we have here in the ship that might help them?"

"Who, Colonel Ashby?"

"The natives of 47 U Maj D."

"Help them in what way, Colonel Ashby?"

"Something I could teach them." Ashby returned to the table and forked a cube of thermostabilized ham. "Their life seems very hard."

Clark said, "Oh, I don't know, Sir. Look at them. They hunt, cook, eat and make fires. Plenty of fresh air."

Tongue shook something yellow off his fork. "Fresh air, my ass."

Ashby gathered the empty trays and wiped off the table. "I know that it goes against the mission objectives to help these people, to affect their proper course of development, but I think we can impart something minor, something they would learn anyway. They don't seem to have a sense of community, which could help them, I think, to accomplish goals."

Erasmus Clark, looking out the window, watched two females empty water sacks into a goat pen, while over by the fire a hooded figure gestured with the Goat Horn man.

Clark sighed heavily and said, "You know, I used to spend weekends in the country when I was a child. My Grandpa's cabin. I used to sit by the creek after lunch and skip rocks for hours. And every day I'd see this same lizard, a little brown one with a black tail. He'd lie in the sun for hours on this same rock. The crazy thing is, I wanted to *be* that lizard. Back in town, my parents were divorcing and I was spending a lot of time out there with my Grandpa, who was great, though he was just Grandpa, and all he did was cook me hot dogs and drink himself to sleep. But every single day that lizard reminded me that it's possible to just consistently and predictably sit there and sun yourself without a care in the world."

When Clark turned around Ashby and Tongue were staring at him.

"What?" Clark said. "Did I say something?"

Tongue grabbed the ivory carving from the console and pointed it at Clark.

"Let me tell you something about that goddamn lizard," he said. "He had one thing on his mind: *How do I not get eaten today?*"

Ashby stood at the ladder. "Should we teach them how to irrigate?" he asked.

Clark scratched his nose and shrugged.

"Holy mother-fucking cow," Tongue said. "Look at this shit."

The three men hovered over the carving, on the base of which were carvings eerily similar to Earth letters that read, **DONIPHAN S**.

-----Original Message-----
From: mathison@olafsonfirm.com
[mail to: mathison@olafsonfirm.com]
Sent: Monday February 6, 2002 10:37 AM
To: Richard Balfour
Subject: RE: White Bull Casino
at the very least it'll scare the mess out of the vendors and make it
difficult for tribe to do business.

-----Original Message-----
From: balfourdick@striblinginstitute.org
[mailto: balfourdick@striblinginstitute.org]
Sent: Monday February 6, 2002 10:13 AM
To: Jack Mathison
Subject: RE: White Bull Casino
yea on the barracudas. n. mex legislature back in session march.
sending out feelers.

-----Original Message-----
From: mathison@olafsonfirm.com
[mail to: mathison@olafsonfirm.com]
Sent: Monday February 6, 2002 9:57 AM
To: Richard Balfour
Subject: RE: White Bull Casino
much appreciated. let's keep the heat on the meemaw trust until the
place is shut down. could we get one of our guys in the legislature to
introduce a bill that says any vendor who provides goods/services to
a casino is disqualified from state contracts? let's send in one of our
barracudas. Can we move on this asap?

-- Emails written by lobbyists Jack J. Mathison and Richard Balfour,
discussing the illegal White Bull Casino in Clovis, New Mexico. Courtesy
of Houston Chronicle's "Inside Slant on Gaming Issue Under Scrutiny;"

May 26, 2004

XXV.

Francine, squatting inside a cage made of birch limbs, gathered peat clods and dry grass around her feet. Above her the clouds, oppressive for days, now showed ominous signs of rain; and with every passing hour her skin tightened and numbed. Nobody had brought the fire offering promised, nor the elk jerky or blackberries from the last hunt, and she'd even been denied the time-consuming task of weaving wattles. She busied herself by watching people work -- the women milking and cleaning and dragging around dead animals, hanging and re-hanging the wigwam insulation; the men in their prolonged, pre-hunt fire ritual (eating up enough time for John LaZar to sneak away to use the Cave facilities) while Hunstiber, in his sloth-skin duster, performed benedictions and scratched his ass with the Spirit Staff.

With the accumulated lichen and moss now padding her feet, Francine closed her eyes and let that long-forgotten name cross her lips again: *Erasmus Clark...* Soon sweet memories drifted through the cracks like dry ice: sitting in Civics class scribbling his name in a three-ring binder, watching him play football and baseball and soccer and Frisbee golf from the bleachers, seeing him at the end of the hall and feeling like she was going to absolutely explode with admiration; living every season, every endless teenage year, with utterances of love stuck in her throat like a gobstopper.

But she was so young then, with no idea how to get a guy to notice her, not privy to the tricks and schemes that turned a distracted and self-obsessed dude into a lifelong, devoted and cavalier boyfriend. So she watched him, year after year, holding hands with other girls, kissing them at dances, looping a finger through their belt loops and riding his skateboard into the sunset, while she carried that longing, setting her depth mark for blissful heartbreak.

Erasmus J. T. Clark. One morning during her senior year she woke determined to catch him at the lockers or the bus stop, where she could drop her books or borrow a pencil or accidentally kick him, affording her an opportunity to reach that level of familiarity where she could smile at him when they passed in the hallways. How painful it all seemed now. When she recalled herself in those ridiculous pleated jeans tucked into fringed boots and the enormous T-shirts she wore to hide her prematurely large boobs – with a belt around the outside of her shirt, no less – she hardly felt surprised that no guy had ever asked her out.

This last ditch effort for Erasmus Clark's attention during senior year, the all-time worst year ever because she lost her contacts and had to wear glasses through Prom and Graduation, not to mention her stupid retainer and the dumb cheerleader tryout routine that got her booed off the stage; this effort was, in fact, a phone call she made around nine on a weeknight. His mom answered annoyed. When he finally got on the phone, she swiftly introduced herself and asked if he'd like to go to the Sadie Hawkins Dance, to which, she learned – like a sock to the stomach – that he already had a date.

He asked, "Are you that girl who did the dance from *Cats*

for cheerleader tryouts?"

"Yeah."

"Want to hear something weird?"

"Sure," she said.

"I have sexual feelings for you."

"Really?"

"Weird, huh?"

"My mom needs the phone," she said.

"Meet me after school by the pole-vaulting pad?

"I don't know."

"Meet me."

"Bye." She hung up.

Her blood boiled the rest of that night and, in the bath, she sunk underwater and screamed so loud her mom could hear her in the pipes downstairs. After school the next day, however, instead of going to the pole-vaulting pad she ran straight to the bus and sat in the way back where she read the first sentence of *That Was Then, This Is Now* over and over again.

Sadie Hawkins came and went, as did Prom and Graduation, and she moved to Santa Monica with her mom, who was a traveling nurse.

• • •

Before leaving on the hunt, Roanoke stopped by Francine's cage. At first he acted rude, so she showed her displeasure by scooting away and baring her front dentures.

He cocked his head and said, "Oo-lahka-Luhk," which was sweet, but not enough to change how she felt about everything. He reached through the bars. She didn't even look up.

Out by the surface path McElroy and the others, with their spears and slingshots and buffalo head disguises, called out for him. He made a rude gesture to Francine before stomping away with his buffalo headdress crooked.

Over by the mud pit Gail was managing the yak herd. Francine hissed until she looked over. Francine gestured, *drink*. Gail checked her back, dropped the herding staff and tiptoed over with one of the goatskin sacks.

Gail stuck the opening through the bars and Francine leaned back to let the water pour over her, though she shivered in the chill. Gail squatted next to the cage. Francine cocked her chin in the direction of the fire.

Gail poked her left butt cheek. *Can't.*

Francine hugged her arms and shivered.

Reluctantly, Gail snuck over to the fire, but the moment she grabbed a flaming twig a nasally voice from the Spirit House yelled, "Natha-Luhk!" She dropped it and ran back to her yaks.

The Spirit House tarp opened. Michelle Skye stood there in thigh-high leggings, a rabbit skin loincloth, a turquoise-vortex bikini and a headdress adorned with little yellow falcon beaks.

Francine said, "Well, I'll be…" under her breath.

Michelle, in an oddly seductive way, sauntered over to the cage, her long legs moving like stilts. She sat on a soft tumbleweed and waved her long nails, enacting a spell of some sort.

"I hope you're conjuring up some Buffalo wings," Francine said. "I'm starving."

"Wish I could let you have some fire, but… orders. Jeffries says you get a miserable day or two in solitary confinement for your nonconformity. Have you seen *Papillon*?"

"Don't start that. Listen, could you bring me the basket I was making, or any kind of half-finished weaving project? Maybe some finger-bone runes?"

"Hang loose one more day." Michelle tugged at her underwire. "LaZar and Jeffries are brainstorming some kind of Punishment Court thing."

"What the hell?"

"They'll probably hang you upside-down or brand you."

LaZar's horn blared from the Chief's tent. Michelle shaded her eyes, looking across the valley at the spaceship, which had begun to rumble monotonously as the ramp lowered from the underside. She made a quick farewell gesture before sprinting back to the Spirit House.

XXVi.

Inside the Chief's hut, John LaZar -- or Kanuda, as he was known among the Uhluk – motioned for Clark, Tongue and Ashby to sit on the ceremonial rug before his throne -- actually the rump of a long-petrified beaver – and waved his concubines to bring the limestone bowls filled with berries, dried grasshoppers and raw liver cutlets.

Clark and Ashby wore blue NASA-issue jumpsuits, U.S.A. ball caps and black boots, while Tongue, clearly annoyed, wore his collared Roman Catholic cassock with a rosary.

Ashby looked around the hut, which had been constructed by thin limbs bent in arches, the ends tied together and reinforced with some kind of lace extending across the dirt floor. On the outside of the frame, animal hides had been hung to provide insulation and privacy. A hole in the roof provided ventilation for the small fire beside the throne.

Kanuda held out his arms. "Kanuda gantala," he said. He pointed to the limestone bowls. "Puya-trala. Puya-trala."

Ashby patted his stomach and shook his head.

Kanuda repeated, "Puya-trala."

Ashby and Clark stared vapidly at the bloody liver cutlets and dried grasshoppers while Tongue's eyes wandered to the topless concubines with bead decorations outlining their nipples.

Clark, with a forced smile, grabbed a handful of

grasshoppers.

Kanuda nodded, impressed. He pointed to the raw liver.

Swallowing the grasshoppers, Clark's eyes glazed over. He reached for a wobbly piece of liver.

Ashby got Kanuda's attention. He showed his empty hands and pulled aside the rug corner, exposing a patch of hard ground. He took a pen out of his breast pocket, raised his hands -- as if performing a magic trick -- and drew a D in the dirt.

Chief Kanuda nodded approvingly.

Ashby next drew an O.

Kanuda nodded again, waving for the holy man to come watch.

Continuing, Ashby drew the letters N, I, P, H, A, N and S, underlining the word with the pen.

LaZar and Hunstiber looked at each other, perplexed.

Ashby pointed to the letter D and shrugged his shoulders. "What means this?"

The tribal elders stared blankly at the letters.

Ashby continued, "This… here. What means? What means this?"

"They're not Mexicans," Captain Tongue said.

Clark pounded his chest to get the liver down. "Maybe you should show him the carving, Sir?"

"I didn't bring the carving. I don't want to spook them."

Tongue yawned. "I don't see how that would spook them."

"I don't want to offend anybody by bringing back one of their gifts." He clicked his pen a couple times. "Now, let's try and be less verbal with each other."

The elders squatted over the letters, their faces pale. Suddenly the holy man pointed at the D and said "Jarathra!" flapping his arms and filling the hut with his underarm stench.

"Means 'Bird', I guess," Clark said.

"No idea," Ashby said. "Ah well." He pointed to the O.

The holy man thought for a minute, crumbling some dirt clods. "Moolah."

"Moolah," Ashby said. "Moolah?" He patted the ground.

The chief and the holy man smiled.

"Must be their planet," Ashby said. "Nice work."

"Or dirt," Clark said.

"Could be."

Ashby was pointing to the N when he noticed that everyone's attention had shifted to the corner where Captain Tongue was kneeling by one of the concubines, fondling her beaded hair and showing off his rosary.

"What are you doing, Captain?" Ashby said, firmly.

Tongue turned and addressed Chief Kanuda. "I…" he tapped his chest, "…want – to -- borrow – one – of – your -- womenfolk."

Kanuda looked dumbfounded, as did the concubine.

"I -- would -- like," he repeated, pointing at the concubine, "the *pleasure*…" he embraced himself and swayed a little, "… of -- this -- woman, please."

"Sit down, Captain Tongue, and that's an order!" Ashby said. "Do you want to get us all killed?"

"Lieutenant, look at these people," Tongue said. "Look at us. What the fuck are we doing?"

"Captain Tongue, get away from those women!"

"Hear me out, Boss: When you look at these people, worshipping animal gods, sleeping on the dirt and working all the damn day for a few rabbits, doesn't it stir something inside you?"

"That is an order."

"Don't you feel it in your blood? *Feel* it." He knocked his head. "That's thousands of years of intellectual advancement begging you knuckleheads to wake up and *dominate*. We can be kings among these people -- gods, even -- with everything taken care of for the rest of our lives. That's what we're here for, guys."

"Captain Tongue," Ashby said, "we are here as representatives of--"

"Fuck that. You don't think all that rocket science and nuclear power was intended to send a few guys a million miles across the universe to take photos and soil samples and mingle. That's a lot of fucking money and a lot of fucking time that brought us here, and if you ask me my opinion I say it's all about mounting this pony and seeing how far it'll ride. Are you with me? Let this opportunity pass and the next thing you know you're back on Earth in an infirmary with doctors shoving fingers up your ass."

"And how do your propose we do that, Captain Tongue?" Clark asked. "Just become gods."

"I say we start by banging these chicks."

Kanuda leaped over the beaver throne, aiming his spear. Captain Tongue hiked his cassock and unclipped the thumb-guard on his TASER holster.

Ashby got between them. "Captain," he said, fuming. "I order you directly to the ship. Put your gun in the hold and wait for me. Do not go near any of the natives, or you'll be quarantined."

Tongue stared at Ashby, disbelieving, but saw no quarter. He put the TASER in his thigh holster, looked around the room once more, and punched open the tarp door.

Ashby put his hand on Kanuda's spear and bowed.

He turned to the concubine. "I'm sorry," he said. "I'm sorry to everyone. And I know you don't understand me, but please feel my apology." As he turned back around, he found himself locked in a pungent embrace, Chief Kanuda's goat horn pressing hard against his sternum.

XXvii.

Captain Tongue stomped past a group of natives groveling in the muck, digging pointless holes and, for all he could tell, banging little rocks against bigger rocks.

Though he had expected this kind of underdeveloped prehistoric situation on the ground, 47 U-Maj D was nevertheless for him a big fat stinking disappointment. Against all vestiges of common sense he'd spent his lonely nights in quarantine back at Goddard – when he couldn't bear another covered-bridge jigsaw puzzle – kicking back and dreaming of an elaborate scenario in which the access ramp opens upon a throng of corn-fed babes without a shred of modesty, bearing garlands which they strewn in a path to platform chairs. Carried through the awestruck throngs, who admiringly throw pelts and parchments and undergarments for that matter, he and his colleagues look down upon a bewildered people who sense the true wonder of their arrival, the power of their intellect, the relative cleanliness of their bodies. After a ceremonial meeting with tribal leadership who pretty much bow down and bequeath power to them, they are taken to separate torch-lit bathing pools by their most bodacious female attendants. A feast of some sort follows. They are toasted by the court, entertained by dancers and jugglers and midgets, and eventually led away to beach-side bungalows containing a very hot -- or several hot – female entities with long hair and shell necklaces and if possible knee-high boots. And somehow over time, communication with Skylab gets lost. They get stuck there. And the natives, though intelligent enough to leave them alone for the most part, would find all their knowledge (of whatever they knew exactly; like how to build birdhouses out of license plates) to be extremely useful to their society. He and his colleagues would split the entire dominion into three equal parts, and become founders of prodigious dynasties. And having completely relinquished the numbing pull of Earth's force, they would live a life of constant pleasure, merriment and hilarity, hoping to sweet God NASA didn't send a reconnaissance group to rescue them.

Tongue passed the borders of the campsite. Halfway to the VITRIOL, one of the ugliest creatures he'd ever seen – a vulture with a scraggly, red wattle – crossed his path. Out of frustration he kicked it. It honked loudly and heaved into the air, across the flat and over the ship's RAM-scoop funnel, where it perched and folded away its dirty wings.

"Travel a million miles," he said, "and you still find ugly-ass shit."

He turned back to the campsite. A thin line of smoke curled out of the chief's hut, loosening over the valley. Above the cliffs he saw a shape, a shadow. He grabbed his mini-binoculars and focused, his mouth opening slightly, his heartbeat in his ears. As much as he tried to rationalize, there was no question what he saw: the hairy body, the yellowed tusks, the curling trunk. It turned slowly and disappeared from view.

The moment T. W. Tongue stepped inside the access chamber he sensed something, or smelled something, that recalled the years he'd spent growing up in Queens and riding the New York City Subway: the pervasive and unmistakable stench of underarm rot.

He flipped the thumb guard on his TASER. He squeezed the handle, his finger in the trigger hole, and tried to rationalize this stench that was beginning to take on a weird barnyard element. He entered the hold -- a narrow hallway leading to a small octagonal corridor that opened onto four other rooms -- and peeked into the mess closet: nothing. After the recreation room he checked the short hallway, the latrine, and the equipment room: nothing.

He returned to the recreation room, breathed in and breathed out, and soaked up the silence. He slipped the gun in his thigh holster. Just as he secured the thumb guard, there was a loud thump behind him. He turned to see a nasty looking native – the dirtiest he'd seen so far – jump down from the cockpit ladder hole, a buffalo headdress awkwardly on his head, his arms out for balance, holding the carved ivory object in his left hand.

"Holy Motherfucking Shit!" Tongue yelled.

The native tried to crawl back up the ladder, but Tongue drew his TASER and shot, sending a small, highly charged stringed hook into the creature's neck. On impact the native's headdress popped off and his body contorted. He slammed up against the ladder, his hands clinging to the rungs and, with his last moment of consciousness, said, "Ouch."

XXViii.

Sharise, Jeffries and the Mountjoy Twins huddled in the conference room with *EMU Staff & Volunteer Profiles* files scattered across the table

Mabel chewed on a Twizzler, passing pages to Travis.

"Listen," she said. "I don't know if we're going to find the smoking gun or what, but the integrity of *Operation EMU* is being compromised and I need to know who's accountable."

Sharise -- wearing a maroon Quaker dress and bonnet -- said, "Kids, that would probably be you."

"It's true, you know," Travis said. "*We* recruited Francine. *We* did the background check. But background checks often fail to deliver that level of quality info. Do you remember if you did a polygraph, sis?"

"What the hell would I ask in a polygraph? We had preliminary stats. Did anyone do cross check, field investigation? I don't think so."

"Come on, Mabel." Sharise tucked back a lock of the girl's hair. "You had Clark's stats, including records that he attended Edwin Meese High in Kansas City, the same school Francine attended."

Mabel tossed her brother a folder. "See if any of the dates are wrong. I know this is not our fault. I know it, I know it, I know it!"

Travis scooted over to Jeffries. "Out of curiosity, what's your plan with Francine?"

Jeffries said, "Lemme see," pulling out a large walkie-talkie and pushing the emergency call button.

"Yes, sir," Doniphan's voice came through.

"Need the 4-1-1 on Francine's punishment."

"We're trying to instigate a trial and judgment demonstration as soon as those bozos come out of the Chief's Tent."

"Cool. Where are you now, Donnie?"

"Out in the hall."

Jeffries turned to see Doniphan sitting cross-legged on the lounge couch, watching him. "Weird," he said. "How's the mud pit?"

"I'm told soft. I requested softer."

"Soft*est*. And deep. Think Ann-Margret in *Tommy*. Kay?"

"Roger. Out."

Jeffries said, "Now everybody settle down. Far as Weird Astronaut Guy knows, he landed on a planet with a woman who looks like an old girlfriend, except she's wearing a loincloth. *Right on.*"

"They never went out or anything." Mabel sniffed. "She had a fleeting crush."

"There you have it," Jeffries said.

"Great." Travis started shoving papers into a lawn-size garbage bag. "So, Jeffries, can we get Francine's punishment thing going and done, so we can find out what Ashby has planned in the way of helping the tribe and all of that before the skies clear and we need to get these guys out of here?"

"I still don't understand," Jeffries said, "the deal with the skies."

"Think about it for a second," Mabel said. "When that sky clears they'll see our moon, our constellations, our satellites for

God's sake and we'll be royally fucked."

"Mabel!" Sharise covered her mouth.

"I'm sorry Aunt Sharise. I'm irritated."

"So, we got, what…?" Jeffries asked, "a day or two?"

"At the most," Travis said. "When we say go, our guys will go. You just keep your team focused. The astronauts are going to try and teach them something soon. Mark my words."

"Okay, then," Sharise said. "Let's just keep Francine strictly separated from Colonel Clark for the rest of the mission and I'll keep a close eye on the VITRIOL crew. So far, I haven't noticed any suspicions."

"Cool," Travis said, tying the garbage bag.

"Except," Sharise said, "for that totem."

"Totem?" Jeffries asked. "What totem, honey?"

"During the Gift Exchange, Roanoke gave Colonel Ashby his personalized totem."

"He did? Hmm. That's weird. Which one?"

"I don't know which one, Jeffries. But the astronauts have been examining it pretty closely."

"The wooly mountain goat totem?"

"I don't think so. It's long."

"Hmm." Jeffries shrugged. "I wonder which one."

"This one," they heard from the doorway, where a man in animal skins and a buffalo headdress was holding the ivory carving.

"Oh right," Jeffries said. "The Elk Sun Deity mammoth tusk totem. Beautiful craftsmanship."

The hunter lifted his headdress; it was Captain T.W. Tongue. "One of you gonads fetch me a beer," he said, aiming the totem around the table, "while the rest of you better tell me what in the Sam Hill is going on."

To date, the [Meemaw] textile fabric remains a mystery. Though we can identify churro fibers and flannel bolts in the yarns, in addition to fibers like flax, goat and silk, we find unidentified substances absent in the Spanish yarns, Moreno yarns and Navajo textiles. As for the dye process, forensic analyses undertaken at UT-El Paso in 1992 and Rutgers in 1994 determined that the substance they used for centuries of rug making contained a preponderance of human blood.

-- Alexis P. Peebles, "Process and Analysis: Certification of Native American Textiles," Crochet Craftsman, July 2001

XXIX.

Francine, who had fallen asleep watching logs collapse in the bonfire, woke to find Erasmus Clark reaching through her cage.

She scooted away, trying to look terrified. No one was around, so she leaned back and watched him make odd hand gestures that seemed like questions, but she had no idea.

He gestured to the cage and said, "Why?"

She crept closer, touching the cage and her elk shawl, pointing to the Tribal Elder's hut. "Tooluk-Ta! Nano Luhk."

"Tooluk-Ta." Clark repeated.

"Tooluk-Ta! Nano Luhk," she said again, clutching the shawl.

He got out his notepad and started writing. After a few scribbles, he stopped. "What am I doing?" he said, smiling.

Francine pretended she didn't understand; and, to be honest, she didn't.

He pulled at the cage opening and felt around for a latch. She pointed to the pin latch on top of the gate, and the stone stepping-stool on the other side. Clark looked over his shoulder, got on the stone and pulled out the pin.

He moved the stone and crawled inside. Francine motioned for him to stop. She touched his face, tracing his brow, down over his laugh lines, to the nicks on his jaw where he'd shaved.

The boyish qualities she remembered had nearly faded, and for a moment it made her sad, as she realized that that beautiful face she remembered was lost. The more she looked at him, however, it occurred to her that her girlish passion – which still fluttered inside her – had actually been inspired by something unreachable and unripe, unlovable even, and that this face now in her hands, washed up across the heartless years, was the one she'd always been meant to hold.

Her hands moved to the slope of his shoulders and down his arms, her bone cold fingers trying to assume some of his warmth. Through his skin, she tried to feel the last 12 years, as if everything he'd seen and touched and loved -- every far-flung experience and every stretch of lingering boredom -- could come through his pores like the smell of onions. Her fingers spread across his chest, trying to grasp everything and never let it go away, with all of her forgiveness and understanding, these cut-dry creeks that had led him here to this blighted crater, into her arms. He had abandoned his entire life, whatever it amounted to, for this. Or at least he thought he had, which was the same thing.

As she reached his hips, her hand bumped into a big gun.

He closed his eyes. His breathing grew deep.

From the bonfire, John LaZar's goat horn sounded. Clark jumped. "I'll come back," he said, making a hand gesture that seemed to say that he'd be hopping across the desert to see her later. He got up, waved goodbye and ran to meet the other astronaut, who had left LaZar's hut.

Francine pulled her cage shut and stepped onto the rock to replace the pin in the latch. She sat back down, fanned her neck and slid Erasmus Clark's big gun under a bed of nettles.

XXX.

A misty rain had begun, growing heavier as the winds blew, and the astronauts quickened their pace across the valley.

"How did the rest go, Colonel?" Clark asked.

"I presented a few basic scientific concepts about our planet," Ashby said, "but I'm not sure they understood. I really want to help them, Colonel Clark."

"I know what you mean, sir."

"The aggressiveness of the males, the apathy of the females…" Ashby scraped some grasshopper out of his teeth. "The community is going nowhere, and it all comes back to this nomadic way of life. I want them to find a way to carry on with the business of their lives without abandoning the tribal unit."

"Well, sir, that's their phase of development."

"But every living thing must progress to survive. I see no drive, no understanding of the relation between innovation and reward. The males hunt, and they leave behind this pattern of apathy. Everything is being taken for granted – gravity, physics, nature."

"Maybe they're happy, sir. There are some tribes back on our own planet that have avoided the modern pull and kept this simple existence. It must be something they see no need for – the progress."

"Colonel, I can't stand here and have you say that these people are happy. There is something in every creature that keeps their heart beating. Look at you and me: something moves us to go places, be people. We're just not satisfied with simplicity."

"I could be satisfied with simplicity."

Ashby turned back to look at the campsite, the only sound being the heavy drops tapping their jumpsuits. The hunters, covering the fire from the rain, ordered some of the women to blow on the coals. On the far side of camp, the woman shivered inside the rickety cage.

"We need to access the surface path, Colonel Clark."

"Okay," Clark said. "Why?"

"Chief Kanuda seemed resistant when I asked about the road. It could be they worry about us scaring away the animals they hunt."

"I mean, why do you want access?"

"One way or another I mean for us to get out of this crater."

They turned back to the ship and jogged to beat the heavy gusts of rain. Above the VITRIOL's RAM-scoop funnel, several vultures were circling so gracefully they might have been eagles. They landed and settled into a perch, and soon they were examining the valley with the smug authority of gargoyles.

"So, we go out and take some soil samples and come back before dawn?"

"I mean for a much longer excursion."

"I see," Clark said.

They waited while the ship's access ramp made its slow deployment.

"What about the VITRIOL?"

"It's safe here for now."

"And the tribe? This might anger them."

"What are you suggesting, Colonel Clark?"

"I think I should stay, Sir, while you and Tongue go."

"Out of the question."

"I could get the anthropological stats out of the way."

"Colonel Clark, we didn't train for a year and travel millions of miles to land on a planet without setting eyes on it. We have to crawl out of this hole or the entire mission will have been a waste."

Climbing the access ramp, Ashby's heart grew heavy. Captain Tongue's actions back at Chief Kanuda's hut were unconscionable, and he hoped that relations with the Uhluk tribe had not been damaged. As for the captain, if he didn't sense any remorse he would have no choice but to confine him to the hold until they returned to Skylab, where a NASA video tribunal, he supposed, would have to enact disciplinary procedures.

Inside the access module Ashby and Clark pulled off their boots.

Ashby slipped on his traction socks and said, "Colonel, I'm going to deal with Captain Tongue now. In the meantime I want you to prepare our survey equipment and climbing gear. We're hitting the far cliff at nightfall."

Clark nodded, staring at his boots.

Ashby found no sign of Captain Tongue in the hold, where he had told him to wait. He checked the mess module, the latrine and the recreation room: No Captain Tongue. When he climbed the ladder into the cockpit, however, he found a hairy naked man playing chess at the commander's panel.

Ashby stepped away from the ladder portal, allowing an unobstructed path of escape for the native. He clapped his hands, calling, "Whoop! Whoop! Whoop!"

The man sat upright. His head turned slowly, flashing his Cro-Magnon smile. The moment he sensed the clear path to the ladder hole, he was gone.

Ashby went to the window to watch the naked man sprint across the clearing.

XXXI.

While Captain Tongue sat handcuffed in the conference room with the buffalo headdress over his head, the Mountjoy Twins, Sharise and Jeffries sat in the lounge area. *The Seventh Voyage of Sinbad* was playing on the television.

"One thing's for sure," Sharise said, on the couch between the twins. "We can't let this knucklehead back into *Operation EMU*."

On the screen the sails of Sinbad's corsair unfurled, the steering wheel spun and the keel plowed toward a sliver of land in the distance.

"Tongue was always a menace," Travis said.

"Why did you use him?" Sharise asked.

"He fit a profile," Mabel replied. "Good-for-nothing asshole."

They watched as the shore boats lowered and Sinbad, along with a small band of men, rowed their way to the mysterious island.

"I think we can be pretty sure the integrity of the mission hasn't been compromised for Ashby and Clark," Mabel said. "So, let's just move forward."

"Question is how we get Tongue out of here," Sharise said. "I don't trust him staying in the Cave with us."

"Talent needs to figure this one out."

Sinbad leaned on the bow of his boat, a hand over his eyebrows, scoping the soft hills and palms behind the sun-blasted beach.

"I mean," Sharise said. "If we take the hokey approach, Ashby and Clark might suspect something. If we go tragic, they might be too demoralized to continue the mission. Keep in mind they're going to lose a man millions of miles from Earth. That's a lot of paperwork when they get back."

"We have to *kill* Captain Tongue," Mabel said. "I mean, *make it look like* we kill him. I know this Ashby guy. I read his Meyers-Briggs like fifty times. If he thinks his man is alive, he'll do everything he can to hunt him down."

"Jeffries?" Sharise said. "Are you ready to brainstorm Captain Tongue's death?"

"Shh… shhh…" Jeffries, sitting on the other side of Mabel, pointed to the television, where the shore boats were sliding into the sand. "There's a special place in my heart for this one," he said. "When I was a kid they used to play a whole bunch of these Harryhausens every Saturday at the Bakersfield Emporium Theater."

"Wow. That's so cool," Travis said. "And it cost like a nickel, right?"

"Nickel? What the…" Jeffries looked down the couch. "How old do you think I am?"

"Sixty-something?"

Jeffries grunted. "Nickel couldn't buy you shit."

Sinbad and his men set foot on the beach and walked toward a primitive temple fashioned out of a sea cave, lined with an impressive entablature. Within seconds a man who looked an awful lot like Albert Finney as Daddy Warbucks in *Annie* scurried out, followed by a giant, disoriented, Clay-Mation

Cyclops.

"Kill him! Eat him! Kill him!" they heard a voice behind them.

They turned to see Bernice, the Props lady, pumping her fist, a length of rope around her shoulders.

"Pardon," she said, walking away.

XXXII.

"DORC, do you read?" Ashby checked the commander's panel switches. "Are you okay?"

The blue screen's pattern rippled. "Yes, Colonel Ashby. I am unharmed."

"I am glad to hear that. Now, I need to ask you a few questions."

"Proceed."

"How did that 47 U Maj D native access the VITRIOL?"

"The hatch was left open, I believe."

"Don't the doors close automatically?"

"Not when they've been left open."

"Huh?"

"I don't understand the question, Colonel."

"Never-mind." Ashby ran a functionality test on the radiation meter and the roving high-gain antenna. The panel seemed intact, with all settings normal, the pens and notebooks and all other paraphernalia untouched; which seemed strange, considering that the entire room and its contents must have been a real spectacle for someone who had seen nothing all his life but the stark natural world. Though he was grateful the man hadn't done any damage, it might have been interesting to see what, if anything, had piqued his interest aside from the DORC monitor.

"What can you tell me about that native man?"

"Not very much, Colonel Ashby," DORC said. "He took my bishop."

Ashby's chin dropped. "I left you and the VITRIOL exposed. I'm sorry."

"No harm done, Colonel. Incidentally, there are some poker glasses in the first aid cabinet if you want to play a quick round of Texas Hold'Em."

The rain swelled outside, tapping against the broken window's plastic covering.

"DORC, my next question concerns Captain Tongue. Can you locate him?"

"Checking the cabins... Checking vicinity... No sign, I'm afraid."

"Strange. He did come back here, yes?"

"Affirmative."

"And he left again?"

"Colonel, I am feeling unnecessarily put-upon."

Clark climbed the ladder. "Found these, Sir," he said, putting Captain Tongue's jumpsuit, underwear, socks, boots and TASER on the table.

"God almighty." Ashby squeezed the back of his neck. "Just one native entered the ship, DORC?"

"Roger that."

Ashby stood up and scanned the cliffs for a shape, a moving sign, anything. "Colonel Clark, I think we have an AWOL."

"Sending an alert to Tongue's beacon," Clark said, entering Tongue's coordinates on the console. "Wherever he is, he's naked. I checked the access module and his other gear is intact."

"The other man was unclothed as well," Ashby said, flinching. "Strange."

After sending the beacon Clark pushed away from the console and looked through the window. It was twilight, but the rain hadn't stopped, and wisps of smoke curled out of the huts. Meanwhile, on the far side of the village, the imprisoned woman sat in her cage, hugging her knees. He couldn't decide what amazed him more: that they were punishing her for not revealing her body to the astronauts – and he was certain now that was the issue – or the fact that she had the courage to defy the tribal authority in what was surely a high-pressure situation for all of them. Why such an emphasis on showing their breasts? Maybe the tribe considered them powerful symbols of fertility or female beauty. And why had this particular female gone against form? She had a special kind of courage, he thought, the kind that could change the developmental course of a species.

A beeping noise sounded.

"Colonel Ashby," DORC said. "I'm getting a signal from Captain Tongue's beacon. It's coming from the surface."

"Jiminy Cricket," Ashby said. "Location, please."

A 3-D map of the valley flashed on the screen, showing a blinking light beyond the cliff's edge.

"Colonel Clark, get our rain gear. DORC, un-dock the surface rover."

XXXIII.

After the heavy shower, the rain turned to a drizzle and the clouds thinned, allowing a faint glow upon the valley. The wind, which had been damp and cool for hours, now mixed with humid gusts. The natives ventured out of their huts to survey the soggy mess.

Francine shivered in her cage, working her wrinkled thumbs around a small basket-in-progress. She tossed it aside and dug her thumbnails into the birch wood bars to watch Hunstiber do squats with his Spirit Staff. Over by the fire Gail swiveled the fire stick in a mound of ignitable grass -- a thing she did for a few minutes before sneaking the waterproof matches out of her leg wrap and lighting the kerosene-treated L.L.Bean fatwood. Roanoke, meanwhile, sat on a rock and shivered in an elk-skin duster while Michelle applied an ash and mud concoction to the TASER wound on his neck. Coming down the surface road the hunters marched single file with a wild boar on a pole.

Francine shifted sides to watch John LaZar confer with a hooded man by the Chief's Hut. The hunters interrupted them to show off the boar, which they all admired for a moment before LaZar ordered his concubines to the mud pit and the hooded man stole off toward Francine. Soon he was sticking his face between the bars, lifting his hood and wobbling his eyebrows.

"Fucking Jeffries."

"Surprise, baby."

"Get me out of here, you creep.

"Soon enough. We're gonna punish you in about fifteen minutes."

"Then can I go back to my wigwam? You have no idea all the shit I have to do before it gets dark."

"Now, I want you to think on a couple of key words for your character."

"Are they *boobs* and *tits*?" Francine flipped back her soggy hair. "Just tell me what's the punishment."

"The words are *cooperation* and *compliance*, baby. It's what makes the world go 'round. One other thing." Jeffries peeked over his shoulder. "Stay away from Weird Astronaut Guy."

"Erasmus?"

"We're about to ship his buddy to Guantanamo Bay, so we only got two flyboys left and we're just days, baby, *days* from getting out of here and starting work on *Slow Death*, a real goddamn picture with *decent* catering."

Francine shivered. "What's the punishment?"

"*Cooperation,* okay?"

"Stop it."

"*Compliance?*"

"I will kick your ass, you little African-American shrimp."

"Good girl." Jeffries took off in the direction of the campfire, bumping into the yaks along the way.

Gail, after watching her herd scatter, sat on a rock and wiped under her eyelids, her hair clinging to her shoulders like asps.

Francine whistled. She slapped her cheek and nodded: *Are you okay?*

Gail shook her head.

Francine made a broad sweep across the sky: *The sun'll come up tomorrow.*

Gail shook her head again.

Francine covered her heart with both hands: *I promise.*

XXXiv.

Clark and Ashby fastened field utility belts over their pressure suits and watched the Surface Rover – a cross between a golf cart and a dune buggy – lower from the underside storage hatch. When the clamps unlatched Ashby got in the driver's seat. Clark removed a flatbed trailer module from the platform.

"DORC, do you read?" Ashby said into his headset. "Need a systems read."

"Fuels cells are charged, Colonel," DORC responded. "Shock absorbers, data camera, front and back lights fully functional."

"High- and low-gain antennas synchronized?"

"Affirmative."

"Captain Tongue's beacon locked on radar?"

"Affirmative."

Clark connected the flatbed and stuffed extra first-aid gear in the specimen bags. He got on board, raised his thumb and Ashby shifted the controller. The rover thrust forward with minimal noise, heading toward the right side of the village. It bumped over several rocks, dodged a giant tortoise, soon reaching 40mph; and it was then that they noticed a team of hunters coming fast from the bonfire.

Ashby shifted into high gear. He took a wide berth. When he cut hard to the surface road the hunters formed a blockade at the incline. Ashby accelerated with the hope that they might scatter; instead, they knelt with their spears out. Several feet away Ashby slammed on the brakes, making Colonel Clark fly over the high-gain antenna and land face-first at the natives' feet.

Ashby whipped out his TASER. "Talk to me Colonel," he said through the headset.

"No worries," Clark said, helped up by the natives. They led him toward the campsite, waving for Ashby to follow.

They came to a mud pit situated between the thatched huts and the giant rock. At the head, on stones shaped curiously like recliners, Chief Kanuda and the Priest sat surrounded by their concubines. The hunters and native women filled out either side of the circle, cross-legged on crude woven mats.

Clark and Ashby were shown to a pair of awkward stones on the far side of the pit. It wasn't until they had taken a seat and leaned on their helmets that they noticed the woman in the elk-skin shawl. She stood in the center of the mud pit, her hands tied to a rope that wound through the slop and into the hands of Chief Kanuda.

Kanuda tugged at the rope. The woman stumbled forward. He severed her bonds and said, "Tooluk-Ta – Nada Luhk!" in a voice that seemed angry, disappointed and slightly aroused.

Clark whispered, "I think I know that word, Colonel. It's what happened during... She-- "

"Quiet." Ashby cringed. "Don't get us killed."

Chief Kanuda waved his spear over the woman. After some ominous chanting, he cried, "Valla-Jo-Valla!" and pointed to a yonder wigwam.

The tarp was opened by an exotic-looking woman the astronauts hadn't seen before, her statuesque figure wrapped in a silky patchwork of lynx or mink. She stared across the valley for a moment, until the wind ceased and everything settled into a confusing silence. Kanuda blew the goat horn again, and she took measured, ceremonial steps toward the pit, eventually making her way to the edge. She turned to the elk-skin woman and, in an obvious gesture of intimidation, removed her lynx covering to reveal a woven bikini ornamented with polished crystals. With curious grace, she slid two rib bones from behind her head and let her hair cascade, maintaining an erect posture with her chest protruding and her arms curved, like a game show fixture. She dipped her toes into the pit and began to rhythmically slosh. The hunters clapped along with her heavy churning.

• • •

Before Francine even had a chance to process the outrageous spectacle of her sometime-co-star's outfit -- especially the stunning turquoise-studded wire bikini that she hoped to get a chance to try on at some point -- she found herself under attack. After dodging a swift lunge for her shoulders, Francine moved quickly aside, got low under Michelle Sky's waist and hoisted her into the mud.

The hunters cheered.

In long strokes across her arms and legs, Michelle shed a heavy layer of mud. Francine crouched, waiting, with a wide wingspan. Michelle came back and they locked arms, dropped to their knees and tipped over. Michelle shoved Francine's face in the slop.

The hunters pelted Francine with dirt clods.

Michelle got up and waved her fingers – a fairly standard tribal taunt -- swaying her other arm and maintaining a decent low-center-of-gravity. Francine, kneeling, wiped mud from her eyes and glanced quickly at Gail, who was shivering on the mat next to Roanoke.

Francine got in her stance again. Michelle lunged forward. Francine pivoted aside and, as the sorceress passed in a waning dive, Francine leveled her with a scissor kick, pinned her down and pulled her arm back. Michelle squirmed loose and again they were roving, and again the dirt clods flew.

The crowd noise quieted as Michelle attempted a sideswiping kick. She slipped and fell hard on her hip, and as she got on all fours to get up, Francine got behind her, reached under her waist and lifted, but Michelle swiveled and hooked her legs around Francine's hips, hanging under her like a baby gorilla.

And it was in this moment, this death-lock -- when Francine raised her fist to deliver the decisive blow -- that Michelle reached for Francine's neck, slipped and grabbed onto the elk-skin shawl, tearing it away as she fell.

• • •

A patchwork of baffled squares had formed in the thinning cloud and, from a far corner of the western sky, a scaly redness appeared like an outbreak of hives. A bevy of sage grouses moved across this broad dome and Francine stood – at least to the speechless crowd – as an axis unto herself.

Michelle, leaning back in the mud, was, like everyone else, completely unable to take her eyes off of her.

With her arms curved and her right leg forward, Francine looked like a statue in a lonely European square, frozen in dubious glory and ruined by the elements. Below her shoulders, which sloped like cables on a suspension bridge, the contour of her breasts rose slightly into peaks that looked like swollen, half-submerged pomegranates while, down below the loincloth, her thighs bulged like a pair of upside-down canoes.

What the men saw here was a body that – like it or not – they had probably seen long ago on a drug store paperback: a female body, to be sure, that either fought a dragon, or rode a dragon or struggled in the clutches of a six-armed creature; but what they had always loved about this woman -- the weight and power and definition of her flesh, the brazen nakedness, her mastery of fear – was a representation of what they had always wanted to be themselves: a protector and a lover, unrelenting in punishment and bountiful with rewards. For the women, however, Francine's nakedness implied something completely different. She had become one of those people who, no matter how you looked at it, would never be the same. And the overwhelming effect of her body came from the fact that she was no longer just an object of sexual consideration, but now transformed into something nurturing and motherly; to be exact, pregnant, and into the beginning of her second trimester.

• • •

Colonel Clark had hardly taken in the enormity of this scene when the victorious woman whistled to a female observer who reached in her goatskin bag and -- to his utter shock -- tossed a TASER stun gun across the pit. Immediately the hunters' wives grabbed the spears, got behind the men and, in a move that had obviously been planned, tucked the blades under their hairy necks. With the men contained, the half-naked mud-caked woman stomped toward Kanuda with the TASER aimed. When she got there she ripped off his goat horn, slipped it around her neck and gestured for his ceremonial robe. With an ashen face, he removed it, along with his headdress and, reluctantly, his jagged spear. After she had covered herself in his robe and fastened the headdress, she waved the gun at the Priest, who flinched behind his Spirit Staff.

Meanwhile, the hunters bowed with their hands raised; soon, it seemed, all the males understood that a change had been made. They pressed their foreheads on the wet ground, and stayed there until well after the females had returned to their huts, and the once-imprisoned woman – now their chief – retired, freshly clothed, to her petrified beaver throne.

XXXV.

"Take it easy, guys," Doniphan said, pouring two cups of coffee from the samovar.

John LaZar, in a smoking jacket and Dockers, twiddled his thumbs at the conference table while Hunstiber leaned against a strategic map of Granada.

Doniphan handed them coffees. "You're not used to this kind of thing."

"Not used to this kind of thing?" LaZar gestured with the coffee, spilling a glob. "You mean like, the whole nature and course of the production just changing like that?" He sipped. "No, I'm *not* used to it. And, to be honest, I want Jeffries in here right now. I consider myself done with this project."

"And I would like this matter cleared, as well," Hunstiber said. "I have to go out there at some point and perform the chiefly benediction; that is, if the coup stands."

A humming began in the hall, growing louder, and Jeffries rolled into the conference room on a Segway. He parked it in the corner, removed his helmet and got a cup of coffee.

LaZar tapped the table. "Jeffries, I won't stand for this. What good are my concubines and the mighty Uhluk hunters if some mud-wrestling chit of a girl can just up and overthrow my authority?"

The director poured milk in his coffee, stirring it with a Bic pen. "My question to you gentlemen is, *What the fuck are you doing here?*"

"Where are we supposed to sleep?"

"Bunk in Roanoke's hut. That man needs some fellowship."

"I won't," LaZar said. "I've got the top billing, I've got the track record and I'm not sleeping in a hunter's hut without my concubines."

"You are and you will, my friend."

LaZar paced in front of a glass-encased model of the U.S.S. Ticonderoga. "I'll lead a new coup and reclaim my throne."

"No way," Jeffries said. "We got a story to tell, and this story has changed course. Get back out there and endure another day of it. The astronauts are leaving pretty soon and we have other scores to settle and plot lines to follow."

"But it doesn't make sense," Hunstiber said. "Sociologically."

"Exactly," LaZar said. "Prehistoric people wouldn't stand for this behavior."

Jeffries sat next to Doniphan. "I want everybody to take a lesson from the late Russ Meyer."

"Not a good idea," LaZar said.

"Hear me out, people." He cleaned his glasses with a bandana. "Remember the scene in *Beyond the Valley of the Dolls* where our very own Mr. John LaZar here – playing the unforgettable Ronnie 'Z-Man' Barzell -- straddles Cynthia Myers on the bed and sticks the gun barrel in her mouth and the next thing you know his shirt is off and he's feeling himself up and he's actually a woman, or half-woman, and then – *boom*!?"

There was silence around the table.

"No one remembers that scene?"

LaZar scoffed. "*I* don't even remember that scene."

"Well, good people, *that* is what I'm talking about. There are inevitable turns in life, just like in stories, and we've all got our hands on the Ouija, so let's go out there and give matriarchal living a chance."

Bernice knocked on the door, holding a remote control box with a six-foot antenna. "Mr. Mongo is ready, Mr. Jeffries. Are you?"

Jeffries slipped on his glasses and raised both thumbs. "Make-Up finished with the prisoner?"

"Yah, yah, yah," Bernice said. "He looks nice and bloody."

XXXVI.

Clark and Ashby, still sitting by the mud pit, watched the hunters cower for a good fifteen minutes. Eventually the hunters got up and toted their wild boar to the fire, sneering at the women who guarded the chief's hut.

The vanquished woman with the interesting outfit still lay sprawled in the mud. She soon pulled herself to standing and, beginning at her shoulders, wiped the coat of mud off her arms, her stomach and in long strokes off her legs, maintaining a kind of graceful balance. With most of the mud gone -- only a thin film remaining -- she sat on the recliner stones, crossed her legs and wrung out her hair. When finished, she slopped out of the pit and sneered at the astronauts.

"I guess," Clark said, "it's not a good time to ask for a stool sample."

Ashby stood up. "Now we know what happened to Captain Tongue's TASER."

Clark reached for his thigh holster. "I'm missing mine, too, Colonel. Just noticed."

Ashby looked over at the Surface Rover. "I want to try something," he whispered, handing Clark his stun gun. "Might be risky. I want you to stay here and test the soil, put rocks in your collection bag, fill a gas analysis collector for atmospheric tests--"

"Grunt work."

"Exactly. Act normal."

Clark nodded at the chief's hut. "I thought I should maybe pay our respects?"

"Don't even think about it." Ashby poked Clark's chest. "That woman has a stun gun and I can't afford to lose two people. Stay out here and take samples."

"Where are you going, sir?"

"Captain Tongue is out there somewhere. As his commander I owe him a chance at survival."

"I wish I could go with you and help," Clark said, catching a yawn.

"Better that you stay here."

"Okay." Clark unhooked a core sampler from his utility belt and dropped it, along with his gas analysis sample container. Ashby pretended to help him screw the core sampler into the dirt, then suddenly ducked low and scampered away, quickening to a jog around the bleating yaks.

One of the hunters yelled, "Ayacha! Ayacha!"

Ashby sprinted, as well as he could in pressure boots, in the direction of the Rover. Once in the drivers' seat he slammed the hand controller. The Rover bumped forward, heading up the surface road. The wheels hugged tight and picked up speed, swerving around the larger rocks and over the rain grooves. Fast behind him he heard the natives howling, running. Ashby stared ahead, focusing on the surface, the thinning sky, the mysterious planet waiting at the end of the trail, and his crewmember -- Captain Tongue -- wherever he was, whatever mess he had gotten himself into.

A towering shadow blocked the horizon and forced Ashby to slam on the brakes. The Rover skidded, swerved and stopped.

The natives, equally stunned, hung alongside the Rover.

"Galooginah!" they yelled, and ran back down the incline. Ashby, releasing the hand controller and letting the Surface Rover drift back, watched what appeared to be a giant Koala bear body-slam a naked Captain Tongue.

XXXVii.

"A giant what?" Sharise asked, framed by the VITRIOL video-conference screen.

"Enormous," Ashby said distantly, sitting at the commander's panel, scratching the stubble under his chin. "Thing."

"Ultra-violet surface readings," DORC said, "indicate the creature has three fingers and toes, long front limbs, neck mane and yellow markings on its back. I would surmise this creature is similar to the giant sloth – or *Megalonyx jeffersonii* – that roamed on our own planet in prehistoric times."

"A sloth," Sharise said. "There you go. Did you recover Captain Tongue's remains?"

Ashby lifted a finger to scratch his nose, trembling. "Broke his back."

"Professor," Colonel Clark interrupted. "I didn't see the altercation, but I don't think there are any remains."

"There will be something," Ashby said. "And we'll recover it."

"Of course you will, Colonel Ashby," Sharise said. "However, first things first: The Intergalactic Space Observatory in Vilpsa, Spain, is sighting lower levels of hydrogen outside the 47 U Maj D atmosphere. If we don't take off tomorrow, the VITRIOL won't be able to gather enough juice to make it back to Skylab, especially with all those freakin' vultures nesting in the funnel."

"Tomorrow?" Clark said, looking to Ashby, who had slumped

in his chair. "Professor Vanderslice, *we just got here*. We haven't taken soil samples. We haven't taken any real surveys or notes on the natives." He scratched his thigh under the panel. "I mean, what did we come here for?"

"Fellas, look: You've done so much. You squirted through a black hole and into a different galaxy and landed safely on a planet with threatening *homo sapien*-like beings. You lost a man and it hurts and I don't want any more trouble for the rest of you. It's time to come on back to Skylab."

Clark pushed away from the console and went across the room to stare at the brutal cliffs. "I mean, what do we have to go home to?"

Ashby sat upright, focusing on his panel's knobs and switches. "I'm sorry, Professor," he said. "You caught us at a bad time. What's our ETD?"

"I'm going to program our computer to sync up with your DORC and set a launch for tomorrow afternoon. You are at T-minus 21 hours. That means you and Colonel Clark need to be sedated in your chambers 17 hours from now."

"What about the window?" Ashby asked, thumbing over his shoulder.

"Huh?"

"The broken window back there."

"Oh, crap." Sharise scratched her head. "Go ahead and forget about it."

"Are you kidding?"

"The sunshield visors seal the windows with six-inch titanium steel, with air-tight suction."

"Professor, am I hearing this correctly? You want the VITRIOL to attempt to exceed the planet's escape velocity with a broken window in the cockpit?"

"Well, I hear you Colonel Ashby, but it's not a totally outrageous suggestion. In addition to the visors, the cockpit itself will be sealed at the ladder hole. Meanwhile, you two will be in the sedation module."

"We may never wake up, Professor."

Sharise rolled her eyes. "Okay, Colonel," she said. "If you're really concerned, as DORC mentioned earlier there's welding equipment, bolts and drills and thick sheet metal in the hold. You've got plenty of time to seal the window in the next 17 hours."

Ashby stared at the shadows under his panel. "Colonel Clark, do you read?"

"Don't quit on me, guys," Sharise said.

"Let's do this, then," Ashby said. "Colonel Clark. I need you to get the welding gear from the hold…" he switched off the outside dosemeters and ran a booster endurance search test "…and assist me with exit preparations…" he made notes in the EXIT section of his log. "…Colonel Clark?" he said. He put his pen down. "Colonel Clark?" He swiveled around to an empty cockpit, the only sound the plastic sheet flapping in the broken window. He got up and yelled down the ladder hole, "Colonel Clark?" his voice echoing back.

Search Results: Your event search found 53 Results

1 to 9 of 53 results.

DATE	SALE #	AUCTION	LOCATION	TOTAL
26 Sept 03	MM345	FP Meemaw Mat #34, Stribling Estate	Paris	2,300 EUR
		Session 1		2,300 EUR
26 Sept 03	MM312	FP Meemaw Mat #13, Stribling Estate	Paris	3,866 EUR
		Session 1		2,801 EUR
		Session 2		967 EUR
26 Sept 03	ST209	FP Meemaw Mat #43, Stribling Estate	London	3,120 GBP
		Session 1		3,120 GBP
26 Sept 03	ME567	SP Meemaw Mat #2, Stribling Estate	New York	3,987 USD
		Session 1		3,987 USD
26 Sept 03	MM354	SP Meemaw Mat #31, Stribling Estate	Paris	2,223 EUR
		Session 1		2,223 EUR
26 Sept 03	MM362	FP Meemaw Mat #176, Stribling Estate	Paris	2,092 EUR
		Session 1		1,680 EUR
		Session 2		412 EUR

DATE	SALE #	AUCTION	LOCATION	TOTAL
26 Sept 03	ME671	FP Meemaw Mat #86, Stribling Estate	New York	2,450 USD
		Session 1		2,450 USD
26 Sept 03	MM360	SP Meemaw Mat #37, Stribling Estate	Paris	2,354 EUR
		Session 1		2,354 EUR
26 Sept 03	ST212	SP Meemaw Mat #21, Stribling Estate	London	4,200 GBP
		Session 1		4,200 GBP

--- Auction purchases of the Stribling Estate's collection of 500 Native American Blankets, in one day by an anonymous buyer; courtesy, Sothebys.com.

XXXViii.

A gloomy twilight settled on the valley, making the sage grouses retreat to their VITRIOL perch and drawing the odd lightning bug. Erasmus Clark jogged across the clearing. For once in his life, he didn't care about consequences; like a man who had been standing halfway in a river all his life and one day decided to take his chance with the currents, he was just hoping he came out alive on the other side.

Through the dusk he could see the village settling down for the evening. The hunters tossed twigs into the bonfire and the women – no longer toting water or repairing the animal skin insulation on the huts – now stood together talking, leaning on spears, while the yaks scattered in the valley. Clark took a wide berth and ducked behind a row of stretched animal skins, between two large stacks of twigs and eventually to the chief's hut, where two females guarded the entryway with spears.

Clark bowed. The guards didn't move. He reached for the tarp, but they blocked it with the spears.

"Please," he said. "Tooluk-Ta. Nada Luhk," -- the only words he knew. He had no idea what they meant.

One of the females went inside the tent, returned and motioned for him to enter.

The hut was dark, except for a glowing pile of coals. His eyes adjusted and soon he could see the woman who had consumed his thoughts, sitting cross-legged on the beaver throne, covered in the chief's robe, one hand holding a planted spear and the other resting on a headdress.

She pointed to the rug. "Uhluk Luhk. Oo-oo-Ta."

Without taking his eyes off her, he fell to his knees. He lowered his head onto the rug, without a concern for anything but the will of this creature, whether or not it resulted in the loss of his life.

Soon, he felt her thighs beside him. He reached for her. She cradled his head. When he looked up at her eyes – both sizzling, like genius brains in formaldehyde – he understood that love was not a chemical effect anymore but a real thing from which everything came and to which everything returned; not only more powerful than death, but death itself: all things beautiful and despicable wound into a spectacular black hole roving through the darkness without logic or direction and devouring everything in its path. And life: The masses on Earth whom he had once considered impositions were, in fact, true miracles of existence. And beauty: Looking into these eerily familiar eyes he had no other choice but to believe that a hand had created them – not a biological accident – twisting sinews and forging cells and implanting in the network of thought a sense of hopelessness. This same hand, he believed, had meant for him, Erasmus J.T. Clark, to find this woman on the other side of nothing, for him to believe in this hopelessness, this inevitable accord, this kiss.

XXXIX.

Around nightfall, James McElroy, Roanoke and the other hunters began chanting by the fire, *Alatra! Alatra!*, a threat to sacrificially slaughter the wandering yaks if their demands weren't met -- whatever their demands were exactly.

Soon they came to the Chief's door and demanded an audience. Francine allowed them in. They stared at Colonel Clark, who was snoring in the corner. She blew the goat horn to get things moving.

McElroy smacked his elbows furiously. *Where is our dinner?*

Francine smacked her elbows and pointed back to them. *Make your own dinner.*

Roanoke groaned and pounded his forehead. *Bitches!*

McElroy shook his head. *That's not how it works.* He squeezed his index finger. *Wives make dinner.* He pounded his chest. *We hunt!*

Francine tickled her fingers and made a cutting motion with her thumb. *You have fire. You have knife. What are you waiting for?*

They argued like this for some time until everyone got bored. McElroy drew a circle around his head and raised the back of his hand to her. *You don't have what it takes to be Chief.* The hunters started to file out of the hut, except for Roanoke, who stared wildly at Clark. His breathing grew more desperate.

Suddenly he lunged for the astronaut. Clark woke and grabbed Roanoke's arms, but Francine was already there, her jagged spear tip firmly in Roanoke's ear. He raised his hands. She led him out, kicking him in the ass through the closing tarp.

Clark, still half-asleep, crawled over and rested in her lap. She caressed his eyelids, twisted his hair and quickly checked for lice.

His eyes grew heavy, but fluttered upon hearing a scuffle outside. The tarp opened to darkness and became blocked by the figure of Nimrod Ashby, held back by the female guards, his TASER stun gun waving around.

xl.

"Colonel Clark." Ashby's voice trembled. "I order you to come back to the VITRIOL now."

Francine waved the guards to set him free.

"Sir," Clark said. "I'm having a moment here."

"Our ship is leaving in less than 21 hours."

"Have a nice trip."

"Colonel Clark, you are in for a shit-load of paperwork, or worse, if you don't come with me right now to prepare the ship for launch."

"Lieutenant, I'm in love with this woman."

"Give me a break."

"Do you remember how that feels?"

"You are not in love, Colonel. This is a person of sub-intelligence you've met while on duty as a representative of the U.S. Government."

"She's a woman."

"She's… an individual of the female species. Don't do this to me, Clark. Not here."

"Remember your wife back home?"

Ashby's eyes turned red. "Of course… I do."

"Well, I have nothing back on Earth. Nothing but pain."

"You want to know about pain? Try living here without any penicillin."

"Sir, do you understand what I'm saying? I'm drawn to this. I'm happy. That has to mean something."

Ashby grabbed the doorway flap, catching his balance, as if he were about to faint. "What do I say?" he said, staring ahead.

"Tell them I decided to stay."

"Colonel," Ashby said, turning. "Let me just say…. I've been thinking. People down on earth… when they look up, they're looking at us. Do you understand, Colonel? Which is what makes this --" he pointed at the woman " – all of this … it's a waste. A complete waste."

"Sir." Clark got up. He squeezed Ashby's shoulder. "They are looking up at us because this is where they want to be. This is Paradise. Down on Earth, everything has been staked and decided upon – even people. There's no way I can go back and try to have a relationship with someone who's been socialized to such an extent I couldn't possibly hope to be the one and only object of her desire."

"What the *hell* are you talking about?"

"Sir, Captain Tongue was half right. This is our chance to be reborn. Not to dominate, but to find ourselves. People are looking up at us, so why go back down?"

Ashby pushed aside the tarp. "People always want you to come back down, Colonel," he said, and ducked into the darkness.

Clark turned around to see Luhk sitting cross-legged on the mat. He could sense that she'd felt the conflict of the moment. She held up her hands and he sat with her, touching the half-curls of her hair. As his shoulders sank in exhaustion she reached for him slowly, almost reluctantly, and brought him close, her breaths drowning in a quiet panic as he removed the folds of her garment and lifted her breast into his mouth.

xli.

Early the next morning, Michelle Sky peeked in the Chief's hut. Wrapped in a fur-lined hide, Francine and Clark lay asleep, clutching each other like drowned lovers at the bottom of a pool. She shook Francine awake and made a hurried signal: *We need to talk*.

Francine woke confused. She shook Clark and they kissed dryly. Francine tossed him the goatskin bag and pointed to the door. He slipped on his jumpsuit and left.

Francine gestured to the welcome rug.

"No more hand signals," Michelle said. "I didn't know you were pregnant. I never would have agreed to the mud pit thing."

"It's okay." Francine sat on the throne and wrapped herself in the blanket.

"I never would have agreed in a million years, okay?"

"Don't worry. I'm fine."

Michelle grabbed a bison vertebra from the bone bowl and tossed it in her hand. "So, who's the father?"

Francine sighed. "I'm trying to make some changes in my life."

"Yeah?"

"I can't keep doing what I'm doing."

"So, you don't know who the father is."

"I do. My ex-boyfriend." Francine poked at the smoldering

fire. "He's an investment banker, a great guy. And we had fun for a little while, but I let my emotions get carried away and now everything has changed. Just like everything always does."

"So, he doesn't know you're pregnant?"

"Probably never will."

"Listen," Michelle said, putting the bison bone back in the bowl. "What's going on in here... with the astronaut?"

"You mean like, nookie?"

"I heard he was your high school sweetheart?"

"I had a big crush on him, but never even met him."

"And years later you meet him here as a cavewoman... That's eroticizing."

"I guess." Francine started to clean her nails with a flint borer. "The thing that's bothering me though is I never have any control over things. I mean, being with this guy is blowing my mind, but it reminds me of when I was in high school and how badly I wanted to be... I don't know... the person I wanted to be. Instead, I was this awkward girl, you know: a little too tall and a little too dorky; not especially smart or talented at dancing, even though I tried. But my mom was supportive. Every night she told me how pretty I was, and maybe I was a little pretty but I couldn't do anything to make people notice. I was a lonely kid. I'm sorry. I'm rambling."

"No," Michelle said, squeezing Francine's hand. "Carry on, love."

"Then we moved. Right after high school. My mom and me. To California. And all of a sudden I have this body and people are noticing and it was such a rush, but the wrong things were happening because of it. These movies I've done... I mean, how can I look back on them and feel like I've done anything that has to do with me? Just a month ago I decided that I was thirty years old and I'm finally going to set the tone. And then this happened. See? Now, it's about someone else again."

"This?" Michelle pointed to Francine's abdomen.

"Yes, that, but also *this*." Francine waved at the mat where she and Clark had slept. "It feels like it's about me, but it's not. Once again, it's about someone else – his love, his passion, his needs. My problem is I don't have a passion for anything. So I always fall back on someone else's feelings and how hard it is to keep them interested and stay attractive because everything's so damn fragile. But where's my passion, my needs? Just when I thought I could figure that out and maybe try to follow them... *this* happens." She pressed her abdomen. "See, Michelle? I feel like all my decisions have been made for me already."

"Well, that's life, Francine."

"No," Francine sobbed. "This is not about life. I don't give a shit about life. This is about me." She pulled away from Michelle's grasp. "To top it all off, I'm having sex dreams about people I don't know – people who *may not even exist!*"

Michelle emptied the bowl on the rug and waved her hand over the bones. "What's next then?"

"He says he's devoted to me."

"The astronaut?"

"Yeah. Erasmus."

"In English?"

Francine nodded.

"Then your character has no idea what he's saying."

"But, she feels it."

Michelle studied the bones on the rug. "I see a productive child. I see someone loving you both." Michelle went to the doorway, looking back over her shoulder, "Is this..." she pointed at the sleeping mat, "...your decision? Is this your life?"

"It's just something I have to maintain, you know?" Francine stared at the dusty white coals. "Once again, it's me living someone else's dream."

Michelle pushed open the doorway. "Well, if you're ever going to make a decision it's now. We all have lives to return to."

The tarp fell closed. After a moment, Francine called, "Michelle?"

She peeked out the tarp to see Michelle standing by the bonfire with John LaZar, the hunters and Clark in the dim morning light. They were all watching Nimrod T. Ashby lean over something situated in front of the spaceship, while orange sparks swirled around him like bees.

One of the skittish corn-shuck negroes came screaming out of Dale Hollow Cave waving a lamp. He collapsed in the water by our boat, telling us that he'd seen grandfather's ghost boiling severed heads in a black pot and incanting the spells of cannibal savages. The poor man, bleeding from the head in streaks made purple by the midnight glow, said that grandfather beat him mercilessly with a cane and told him never to breathe a word about the stolen Indian treasure which was, in fact, nothing but the small pouch of gristle and dust we found at the bottom of the glass case in father's study; the very same case that displayed Chief Lark Moon's unsightly, scalp-adorned headdress.

-- Virginia Stribling-Eckerd, <u>The Legend of Dale Hollow Lake</u>, 1879, Stribling Family Histories Inc.

xlii.

"*An* Occurrence *at Owl Creek Bridge*," Jeffries said, standing firmly in the doorway of the Command Center's soundproof studio.

"*Incident*," Yuri replied, sitting in front of his mike station, the thick headphones like a brace around his neck. "*Incident at Owl Creek Bridge*. I remember clearly. *Twilight Zone*. The man is pushed off a bridge, the noose breaks, he runs home to his wife and --"

"I know. I know," Jeffries snapped. "That's not the point we're arguing. It's called *Occurrence at Owl Creek Bridge*. A French short by Robert Enrico."

"You didn't make that clear in the first place, so I win the argument. It's not French."

Jeffries walked backwards, dribbling an invisible ball. "Winner at Cannes..." He faked left. "Starring Roger Jacquet..." He jumped up... "with Anne Cornaly..." He dunked. "...and the TV version was *Alfred Hitchcock Presents*, not *Twilight Zone*." He waved a finger at Yuri and let his tongue hang out.

"Get back on the mike, Yuri!" Sharise yelled from the mainframe panel. "He's entering the cockpit again."

On the video monitor, they watched Ashby scale the ladder with the welding hat visor raised. He went straight for the plastic covered window and smashed it open with a survey shovel, then dragged a plastic tool chest out of a storage closet and began to drop tools out the window.

Sharise leaned closer to the monitor. "What the…" She waved furiously at Yuri, who leaned into the mike and said, "Colonel? May I help you with something?"

Ashby continued to drop the tools.

Sharise ran to the soundproof room's window and waved her hands. Yuri rolled his eyes and nodded. "Colonel Ashby," he said. "What are you doing?"

Ashby hopped from the ledge. "I'm making a rain basin," he said, lowering his welding visor.

xliii.

An hour later, the Mountjoy Twins burst into the Command Center and ordered everyone out except for Sharise.

Mabel pointed at Doniphan, who was lounging by the Air Strategy table playing with a Rubik's Cube. "Get Jeffries," she said.

"He's gone to the village."

"Well send somebody, then."

Doniphan meandered towards the door. As he passed Mabel, she held out her hand for the Rubik's Cube.

Doniphan shoved it in his pocket.

"Please?" she asked.

He dropped it in her hand and left.

"Sharise?" Travis asked. "If you could describe my sister and me with one word, what would it be?"

"Hmm." Sharise wobbled in her swivel chair and thought. "Splendent."

"Splendent?"

"Splendid?"

"Sharise, please," Travis said. "In all seriousness, you know that the word would be 'Results-Oriented'."

"Ah."

Mabel turned the Rubik's Cube over. "Do you know how much this whole thing cost our department?"

Sharise shook her head.

"Three-hundred million dollars."

"Holy cow."

"If we blow this one that's it, Aunt Sharise. CHETO's cash will get turned over to Chairman Chilblain and the other NASA wonks, and Travis and I will wind up doing Led Zeppelin light shows at the Baltimore Planetarium."

"Kids," Sharise said, patting her knees.

They sat on her lap and she hugged them. "We're having a little trouble getting Ashby to focus on the window repair. However, in a mere six hours they'll be sedating themselves and we'll haul them back to the Shacklett Base for observation and I'll take my VITRIOL home for a good cleaning." She mussed their hair. "You kids have done a marvelous job with this experiment, and soon you can get cozy with all that research back at Goddard."

Travis stood and said, "Erasmus Clark is living in the hut with Luhk."

"With whom?"

"Francine Dean."

"Oh, I see. Well, try and get him out maybe?"

Mabel growled at the mixed-up Rubik's Cube and placed it gently on the panel. "The clouds will blow away soon. We have to get those bozos out of there by nightfall."

"I see," Sharise said, glancing over at the video monitor, where Nimrod T. Ashby was driving the Surface Rover toward the thatch village, a big sheet-metal sculpture wobbling on the trailer hook-up.

xliv.

When Francine returned to her hut she found Enoch Jeffries sitting on her beaver throne, wrapped in a hooded cloak.

"Make yourself at home," she said. "Dickface."

"Honeymoon's over, baby," he whispered. "Weird High School Boyfriend gotta get back in his spaceship and *go*." He looked around. "Pretty nice in here."

Francine ordered him off the throne. "Look where your bright idea got you, Macho Camacho." She passed him a platter of dried buffalo brisket.

"Your boobs are way bigger in person," he said.

She began a Threat Display but instead sat down.

"Baby, you're the chief now. And that's cool. But, the chief still works for *me*. Kay?" He took a piece of brisket and smelled it. "I need you to do me a favor and think on your character real quick: What would Luhk do?"

Francine thought for a moment. "Luhk is confused right now. She's queen of her tribe and living with the love of her life, but doesn't know what she really wants."

Jeffries reached into his hood to gag himself.

"Show some respect."

"Ok, your majesty." He sat on the rug. "Need a little insight into where you're going with this; like, on a personal level."

"I'm stumped."

"Look, why don't you do me a favor and kick Fly Boy in the ass? Let him down easy, send him on his way, tell him you're not ready for a life change – I don't know, tell him you caught anthrax from a carcass and you're contaminated for a year – and then, when all this is over you can look him up in the white pages and fornicate in the private sector."

"I don't think that would ever happen. I'm worried about him, Jeffries; all of them. This is a secret experiment. They may get buried in a vault after this."

"Could be. Even so, *you* can't stay here forever."

"Why not?"

"I'm not catching your drift, honey chile."

"This place is perfect for me. I have my house, food. It's simple."

"Too damn cold."

"I can make the fire bigger."

"You need to dry your wattles." He pointed to the roof. "Damp smell."

"Let me finish the stuff on where I'm at, Jeffries, okay? So, here I am, after many years in love-limbo, and a guy I used to have a big crush on shows up and he's being really sweet. He feels that connection, but doesn't know what it is. And that rocks, if you ask me. I'm an animal for all he knows, and lord knows how bad I must smell, but he loves me. Do you know how it feels to be loved for no reason other than you, your actions, your being?"

"Baby, this ain't a Bikram yoga retreat. We got guys with M-16s out there in the flats. You and me: we're just atmosphere. Fly Boy can't possibly buy this too much longer… And you… it must feel like a stupid game after a while."

"I feel like it could go on forever."

"You don't mean that." Jeffries poked at the dirt with an

antler. "Wish I had a frame of reference or something."

"You think too much."

"No, I mean, it reminds me of something. It's right there…" He rubbed his forehead. "I need your help."

"What are you blabbering about?"

"What is this *like*?"

She snapped her fingers. "*Dr. Zhivago*!"

"Go on."

"When Julie Christie and Omar Sharif break into that abandoned house in Siberia and all the rooms are filled with snow, and they find that one dry room and she rests on the couch and he writes poems and they burn spare lumber in the fireplace until the spring thaw."

Jeffries pulled his bottom lip. "B-minus," he said. "Thematically, it's way off."

"Forbidden relationship, forbidden house…?"

"Yeah, baby, but they know who each other are. This here feels a little more like Brian De Palma. Remember in--"

"I got it." Francine kicked his foot. "*Some Like It Hot*."

"Okay. Shoot."

"At the very end when Jack Lemmon and Joe E. Brown are in the motor boat and they do that back and forth about how Jack can't marry him because he can't have children, and so on, and Joe says he doesn't care and then finally Jack takes off his wig and says 'For God's sake, I'm a man' and Joe says--"

"'Nobody's Perfect!'"

"Goddamn you, prick." Francine swatted him with a fleece.

"It's a famous line, baby."

"Get out of here and let me act."

He lowered his hood. "Gonna act yourself right out of *Slow Death*."

"I don't care," she said. "Look at me, boss. I'm finally starring in something -- after twelve years of being strung along -- and now I know how good it feels."

xlv.

James McElroy, Roanoke and the other hunters squatted in the clearing. They were whittling the knots from new birch limbs and fastening the spearheads with strips of animal hide when the rumbling Surface Rover pulled alongside them. Ashby hopped out and unhooked the trailer, which toted something that looked like a hot tub. He dragged the metal structure off the trailer and motioned for the hunters to come closer. McElroy hissed at Ashby, bucking his chin.

Ashby soon managed to secure a small audience of hunters, all squatting and half-paying attention while they put the finishing touches on their spears. Ashby grabbed three long tubes from the sample collection boxes and connected them to a hole in the base of the metal, drawing the tube out in a long line, running about twenty feet. He got a small clamp out of the sample box and showed it to the hunters; then, he clipped it to the part of the tube closest to the basin and proceeded to poke holes in the tube, each about a foot apart.

Meanwhile, James McElroy finished his spear and began to test the sturdiness of the blade. He held it lengthwise and checked the balance, tossed it in his hands a few times and let it tilt on one hand favoring the spearhead side.

Once Ashby had finished poking holes in the tube, he reached under the Rover for a plastic water tank and poured it into the basin.

McElroy noticed Roanoke having trouble with his spearhead strips, so he took it and tightened the slack with his teeth.

Ashby, still emptying the water jug, looked back at the hunters and nodded and pointed into the basin, giving everyone a thumb's up and a crazed smile.

Roanoke took his spear back from McElroy. He felt the grip and waved it around his head like a baton. He checked the whittling work, the firmness of the spearhead and pulled the branch against his knee to be sure the wood wasn't brittle.

Ashby whistled and tossed the empty jug in the Rover. "Rain," he said, pointing at the sky. He kicked the ground and made a cyclical motion with his hands. "Grow." He picked a small weed out of the ground and chewed on the tiny brown leaves.

The hunters leaned on their spears and watched Ashby chew and rub his belly.

Ashby pointed to the basin. "Rain… Save," he said, and while he dug a long row in the ground with a trenching tool, one of the hunters itched his head and bent over for Roanoke to do a quick delousing.

"Now watch," Ashby said, pointing to the basin. "Watch," he repeated. He unplugged the clamp and the thirty or so holes in the tube gurgled sprouts of water.

After a few moments watching the little spouts of water, McElroy grunted, "Chalarata," waving his men to follow him. The hunters hoisted their spears and wandered off in a pack.

"Wait!" Ashby yelled, pointing at the basin.

The hunters turned around.

"Do you people see what this is?"

The hunters' mouths hung open.

"This thing could change your life," Ashby said. "And you

don't care?"

He ran over to McElroy and took his spear. "You don't have to do this every day. You can find other ways to eat. You can grow your food, salt your meat. You can spend more time at home."

McElroy grabbed his spear back. He said, "Chalarata. Uhluk. Chalarata." Then he made some pretty funny hand gestures with regard to Ashby's mother. The hunters laughed – maybe a little too long – slapping their knees and patting each other hard on the back.

Ashby stood mumbling to himself while the hunters went over and sat on the bonfire stones, digging in the dirt with their spears and staring off into the distance while the flames dwindled and sent black plumes into the sky.

xlvi.

Ashby returned to the VITRIOL, stowed the Surface Rover and the trailer and carried an extra piece of sheet metal into the cockpit, where he drilled the four corners around the broken window and sealed the edges with a torch. When he was done, he put the tools away and sealed the hold, latched the meal compartments and locked the pressure suits, boots, helmets and radiation gauges in the equipment lockers.

Back in the cockpit, he sat at his panel and said, "DORC, please raise the ramp and seal the access hatch."

He didn't get a reply, so he grabbed the joystick on the panel and hit the call button. "DORC?"

"Yes, yes, here I am," DORC said. "How may I help you, Colonel?"

"Raise the ramp and seal the access hatch."

"Right away," the computer said. "You realize Colonel Clark remains outside?"

"Affirmative, DORC." Ashby jotted notes in his mission file and stowed it in the safe. "Colonel Clark is not... returning to Earth with us."

"Understood, Lieutenant Colonel. Raising ramp and sealing access hatch."

"ETD, please."

"Launch is T-minus 6 hours."

"That leaves me…" Ashby said, flipping the switch that lowered the high-gain antenna, "two hours before sedation. Please send a signal to Skylab. I'm going to seal the cockpit now, DORC."

"Okay, Nimrod."

Ashby, securing the swivel chairs, paused.

"I mean, Colonel Ashby."

He pushed the window visor button and watched as 47 U Maj D, or what little he'd seen of it, disappeared from view.

He removed two trays from the microwave drawer and sat at the recreation table. He listlessly chewed some thermostabilized turkey squares and sipped a small box of limeade before dumping everything in the compactor chute. Then he prepared his sedation chamber, checked the safety straps, the Propofol IV drip, and the vital sensors.

"DORC, please troubleshoot the biorhythm hard drive."

"Right away, Colonel," DORC said.

"And maybe re-attempt starter jolts to get those birds off the funnel."

"Right away."

"They're toast when the reactors ignite."

"Everything is ready for launch, Colonel. You are T-minus 4.75 hours."

"Thanks, DORC. Thank you for your service. I'm sorry we didn't get much done here, but we got here and that's enough."

"I'm sure we'll work together again some day."

"Possibly." Ashby leaned over his sedation cask, smoothing what would be his bed for the coming eight months. "DORC, I think it's fair for you to know something."

"What's that?"

"We will probably never work together again." Ashby stared

down at the mattress. "I'll still be sedated when we dock at Skylab; and then, if I make it back to Earth I'll be quarantined, checked for any viruses I contracted from this planet, studied, interviewed. There'll be tons of paperwork. And you, DORC: You're the first Operational Computer to land a manned aircraft on a foreign planet with intelligent life. They'll analyze you just as much. They may even dismantle your circuits."

Ashby shut his cask and removed white slipper socks from the airtight linen drawer.

"Thank you for being frank with me, Colonel."

"Least I could do."

"Now, may I be frank with you?"

"You may."

"This whole trip, not once have you accepted an invitation to play me in a game of chess."

Ashby pulled on his socks, smiling faintly. "Alright," he said. "Meet you in the Rec Module in five."

The Las Vegas Meemaws [of the Arena Football League] today made available a news release on a study by Duke University's National Stribling Foundation Survey saying that most American Indians don't find the use of the name or depiction of their "scalp collector" mascot offensive. According to the study, 88 percent said the name does not bother them; nine percent were offended and three percent had no answer. According to the Stribling Public Policy Center, 768 people, who said they were Native Americans, were polled from Oct. 20, 2003, to Sept. 19, 2004.

-- From <u>The Las Vegas Sun</u>, September 24, 2004, "Sports Bites" Column

xlvii.

Back in the Command Center, the mainframe computer programmers stored the last of the back-up floppies and began the process of reverse programming, which would shut-down several large components, including the valley cameras, the cockpit camera, the Jarlsburg Butte radar and some of the audio equipment.

Sharise tightened the belt on her traditional geisha kimono. "Nice C++ work, Archibald." She checked her chopstick hair ornament. "Make sure we don't lose power in the sedation chamber or Rec module. Any word from the Perimeter Team? I want them to snipe those vultures as soon as Ashby goes down."

"None," one of the programmers replied.

"Hmm. That's funny."

"Made two calls."

"Sergeant Philomont?"

"Yup. And the HUMMER scouts."

"Jeez," Sharise said, shuffling over to the soundproof studio, where Yuri sat at his chess screen, his face white as a sheet.

Sharise tapped her watch.

Yuri switched off the mike, and tiptoed to the door. "Almost done, almost done."

"We need him sedated, Yuri. Like, now."

"What am I supposed to do? He's good." He shut the door.

Over by the table map of Tijuana, Jeffries juggled defused grenades while the Mountjoy Twins sat on the floor and watched.

Sharise said, "Everything's on track."

"Cool," Travis said, zoning out on the grenades.

"Only problem is the Perimeter Team. No communication in over an hour. We need the Shawnee 'copter to haul VITRIOL back to Shacklett as soon as Ashby goes under."

Jeffries dropped a grenade and jumped on it. "I have a question, you guys," he said, raising his head. "It's a story question."

"Shoot," Mabel said.

"What happens to Fly Boy in Love?"

"Colonel Erasmus J.T. Clark?" Travis asked. "As soon as Ashby falls under the Propofol spell, we're taking him far, far away."

"Like Branson, Missouri?"

The twins looked at each other briefly and Mabel said, "Nuremberg."

"Oh, man." Jeffries slapped his forehead. "Homeboy's getting flushed."

"There are some very nice facilities there for officers."

"Achtung, baby."

"We have to isolate them, Mr. Jeffries." Mabel tossed one of the grenades. "To ensure the integrity of future CHETO programs."

"And what about 'Dances With Sloths'?"

"Huh? Oh, Captain Tongue slipped a disk. He's being examined at Shacklett and will be sent to Guantanamo Bay after surgery."

Doniphan came in with a bag of ice, scooting an igloo

cooler with his foot.

"Which leaves our only survivor," Jeffries said. "I'm interested in how you're gonna pull this one off."

"That's easy, Mr. Jeffries," Travis said, ripping the ice bag. "We have a simulated Skylab facility back at Goddard."

"Yeah, but what about after that? The script says these guys think a hundred years has passed on Earth."

"Who says he's ever returning to Earth?"

"Travis!" Mabel said.

"It's okay, we can tell him. Mr. Jeffries, Nimrod T. Ashby is going to another planet after this."

Jeffries shook his head. "Another *what*?"

"We don't have the resources, obviously, to simulate Earth 100 years from now, which is how much time he thinks has passed, so we can't take him *home*, so to speak."

"Wait, wait." Jeffries pinched his forehead. "This is too much. You're going to have to pitch it to me."

"Pitch it?"

"Please."

"Okay. Hold on." Travis popped his knuckles. "Okay. While leaving the 47 U Maj D's orbit, the VITRIOL's funneling mechanism fails to gather sufficient atmospheric hydrogen."

"I like it."

"This leads Colonel Ashby through the astral plane and into a parallel universe and having to make an emergency landing on another water-based planet that's almost an exact sister of current-day Earth; in his eyes, a spot-on replica of a quaint, countrified township in the pastoral American South."

"Genius."

Travis tossed the ice bag. Doniphan caught it and did an *alley-oop* into the trashcan.

"We'll take him to Savannah," Mabel said. "Senator Dornanstern of Georgia is not so keen, so we may have to settle with Mobile, Alabama; you know, park him on the outskirts of town, wake him, give him some clothes, let him secretly infiltrate the natives at the Whistle Stop Cafe."

"Game's over," Yuri called from the soundproof studio, looking flushed but relieved. "He's getting in his little bed now!"

Sharise jogged over to the monitors to see Ashby sitting in his sedation cask, applying the biorhythm patches, heart monitors, slipping the IV needle in his arm. He stretched out and strapped his head and arms. "Close chamber, DORC," he said.

One of the programmers tapped a keyboard and the cask's glass cover shut, sealed, and the red lights on the overhead monitor began to blink in a steady pulse.

Yuri, back in his soundproof studio, said into the mike, "Sleep well, Lt. Colonel Ashby." He removed his headphones and shut off the switchboard.

Sharise pressed the folds of her Geisha wrap. "Nice work," she said, shuffling around her programming team with her palms pressed together, nodding repeatedly. "*Operation EMU* is a wrap."

All of a sudden came a loud *Pop!* and confetti shimmered, streamers looped through the room and champagne poured over everyone's heads.

xlviii.

Ashby opened his eyes.

"DORC."

He removed the IV needle, hit the emergency latch and sat up, sucking breaths.

"DORC, do you read?"

Nothing.

He slipped off his traction socks and went to the access module, where he put on a fresh jumpsuit, boots and strapped on his TASER thigh holster. He stood before the access hatch.

"DORC, do you read?" Ashby beat on the door panel. "Open the access portal."

He tapped on the keypad but the lights didn't come on, so he leaned against the door hinge, propped his foot on the other edge and pulled until he had enough room to slip out.

xlix.

Erasmus Clark was drying lichen clumps by the bonfire, listening to the hunters' muttering, when he saw movement on the VITRIOL. It was Ashby, standing atop the access hatch without the ramp deployed, gauging the fifteen-foot fall. He balanced his arms, jumped and landed hard on his hip. He immediately sprinted to the campsite, scattering the buzzards and sage grouses and hurdling the giant tortoise.

When he got to the campfire, the hunters barely looked up.

"I understand now." Ashby fell to his knees.

The hunters turned to him, slightly perplexed but mostly bored.

"Give it up," Clark said. "They can't understand a word."

"Colonel, they're all dead."

"What are you talking about?"

"Everyone we love on Earth is dead," he said, his right hand trembling so much he had to catch it with the other. "I just realized that. I was laying there about to fall asleep and I understood."

"Leave us, Colonel. We're happy here."

Ashby looked at the sky, now moving in thin puffy wisps. A patch of perfect blue had formed directly above him, with a hawk circling inside.

"What have our women done?" he said, hugging his knees

and rocking. "What have they done to us?"

"Don't do this, Ashby. Don't ruin this."

"They have made us nomads."

McElroy put down his spear and looked around at his hunters.

"Go back," Clark repeated.

"You like to hunt." Ashby grabbed McElroy's spear.

The hunters looked at each other, nodding.

"It's what you do. You go out and hunt and return with food and it's what you do. You don't need to stay home. Your wives don't need you, your children don't need you. All they need is the food. The sustenance. You *do* have a life. This is your life. This is your purpose." He tossed the spear back to McElroy. "You are noble."

Clark grabbed all the lichen clumps and crept away from the bonfire, ducking behind a rack of drying spleens.

"Let us together," Ashby said. "Us. We." He pulled out his TASER, and Roanoke hit the dirt. The rest of the hunters fell to their knees. "Let's not pretend anymore. Let's be who we were meant to be, to progress forward, for all of time and forever! Let us reclaim our tribe!"

Former-chief Kanuda appeared from behind the great rock, the holy man at his side. He raised his hands and made a high-pitched, almost singing sound that meandered a little before turning into a deep chant of "Uhluk! Uhluk!"

McElroy made a few hand-signals. The hunters got on their feet, energized, chanting, "Uhluk! Uhluk! Uhluk!

1.

Travis Mountjoy, wearing a tilted party hat, slouched in front of the static Command Center video monitors with an empty champagne bottle hanging off his fingers. Mabel turned and shushed everyone until the party noises ceased.

Travis picked up the black phone. "Mabel, quick, I need Sergeant Philomont's cell."

Mabel read and Travis dialed, saying, "Stupid rotary phone." He listened for a ring. "Shit!" He hung up and looked over at Jeffries, Sharise, Doniphan, Yuri and Bernice, covered in streamers and confetti. "The line's dead."

Sharise said, "We could always go out there and call the whole thing off."

Mabel shook her head. "Three-hundred million dollars, Aunt Sharise, says no freakin' way." She grabbed her stomach. "I'm feeling sick."

"Well, kids," Sharise said, "with all due respect, your three-hundred million is no match for the potential damage to my five-hundred million VITRIOL hydrogen funnel what with all the scraping talons on the titanium filters, not to mention what happens if one of those buzzards falls into the reactor. This really can't go on any longer."

Jeffries, slightly tipsy, put his hand on Doniphan's shoulder. "I don't know why, but this has me thinking about *The Wicker Man*."

"Yeah?" Doniphan said, distracted by Sharise's geisha clogs stomping down the hall.

"Remember when Edward Woodward arrives at that inn on the island?"

"Uh, yeah."

Jeffries drained his champagne flute and burped. "And they show him to his room and it's all snowy out and he opens the bathroom door and finds that woman bathing in the wooden tub?"

"What?"

"You know, she's all sexy and he shuts the door right away cuz he's Catholic or something."

"It's snowy out?"

"Yeah, Holmes. And all through the show he keeps opening doors and finding that woman in the standalone tub."

"*The Wicker Man*?"

"Yes! Jesus, Donnie!"

"Most Honorable *sen sei*, I think you mixed *The Wicker Man* with *The Fearless Vampire Killers*. You know, Roman Polanski walks in on Sharon Tate? You don't see anything, unfortunately, just bubbles. In any event it's never snowing in *Wicker Man*."

Jeffries convulsed with another burp. "Are you shitting me, Donnie?"

"Call me Doniphan, please. And no. No shitting. Edward Woodward *does* walk in on a woman in a standalone tub in *Wicker Man*, but that's just random. You know, near the end, when he's going door-to-door in that Punch & Judy costume."

"*The Fearless Vampire Killers*?"

"Yup."

"My God."

"It's okay, boss. It's been a long shoot."

"Polanski?"

There was a loud bang as Travis smashed a phone receiver against a desk.

Turning around, Jeffries, Bernice, Yuri and Doniphan saw the twins locked in another staring match; and though not an uncommon thing, everyone sensed a new, rapturous edge. Travis and Mabel moved closer, gradually, like the bones of dead lovers searching for each other through the earth, the twin's bodies taking shape and their heads turning into a squirming and agitated kiss.

"Sharon Tate," Jeffries moaned, staring into his empty glass. "That is not good."

li.

Erasmus Clark ducked into the chief's hut to find Francine sweeping the dirt floor with a plume of ratty falcon feathers. He grabbed her spear and handed it to her.

Francine leaned on the spear and watched Erasmus lace his boots. Though she hadn't lost the love buzz, she still felt the inevitable change that occurs when a beginning gives way to practicality; like, matters of reinforcement. Sadly, it had occurred to her that the only way she could keep everything spinning – which was really just a matter of keeping him satisfied – would be for her to expose him, dominate him and crush him. In high school she had neglected the silent treatments, the hot and cold affections, the chesty postures that could have transformed Erasmus J.T. Clark from a self-absorbed, wayward boy into the man he could be; namely, hers. And now the truth was frighteningly clear: She could use what she had – her body, her ability to make people feel good, whatever – to reach a higher level of existence. It didn't matter how she got there. It didn't matter that the power would only feed itself. And it didn't matter that life was hard and ruthless, with nothing to fight the chill but a dusty warmth the world called Love, but should have called Fear. And, to be honest, she wasn't exactly sure what she meant by that.

She opened the tarp. By the bonfire the hunters, ruddy faced and agitated, stood with Kanuda and Hunstiber and the other astronaut. They all seemed to have regained their pizazz.

Erasmus squeezed her shoulder. "We must fight."

She reached back for his hand.

"I will take out Ashby with my gun. Once the hunters see this they will scatter."

Francine slumped. Jail or no jail, this was a good time to call the whole thing off. She could simply say his name, or anything at all, and the spell would be broken and they could all go home and take their chances in the real world. Maybe she and Erasmus could meet for a drink, and maybe this passion, or whatever they had, could resume without any gimmicks – without her wearing loincloths on camping trips and stuff. But, regardless, they should let go and be alone for a few months until nature took its course and her baby came and she had someone else to create illusions for.

"The effect may not last long," Clark whispered, his breath warm and somehow minty. "But these *repeated displays of dominance* are all they will understand."

She turned around and, surrounded by the plumes of burning rhododendron, she found herself looking at the teenager she'd known many years ago – the one who wrestled kids on the field during recess and slammed his locker shut; who got dragged by the back of his pants by the Vice Principal, who kicked the winning field goal when they won State; and, how could she forget, the one who stood outside the gym after Sadie Hawkins kissing Mary Lee Clarkson so hard it made her -- Francine – unable to breathe. It was this young face, thin and smooth and blazing, that she held in her hands, while the words *repeated displays of dominance* chimed from somewhere.

She opened her mouth and kissed him in the most devastating twenty-first-century fashion, their lips pressing together like inner-tubes under a dock: deep and desperate and diffuse.

lii.

The Uhluk hunters, Kanuda and the holy man formed two rows behind Ashby. The natives in back raised their spears. Those in front buffered theirs, planting them outwards. Something about the organized symmetry of this display added to Clark's discomfort, as if the natives – under Ashby's tutelage – had taken on a cold mechanical symmetry. When he looked across to his commanding officer, he understood what that inhuman callousness felt like; he too had decided to kill; and like being wounded in battle, he couldn't feel it all entirely.

Luhk blew the goat horn and the womenfolk arrived, including the sorceress in a rawhide tunic and what appeared to be bearskin knee-highs. None of them seemed particularly threatened by the hunters' alignment, until they saw the look on their leader's face and realized that another monumental change was underway. With zero urgency – and, in the case of the sorceress, a slouching ennui – they formed a line around Luhk, with Clark up front, serving as the counterpart to Ashby, beginning a march across the fifty feet of brush and tumbleweed and yak hair that separated them. As if in a rousing barn dance, Ashby and the natives matched the pace of their adversaries, closing the gap with every beat.

With fifteen feet separating them, Chief Kanuda suddenly wormed through the crowd yelling, "Uhluk! Taloo-ta!" Both sides waited while the former chief rambled for five minutes, hardly disguising a nervous quiver, in what appeared to be some sort of pre-battle pep talk. Luhk felt compelled to do the same, coming out in front of the women to tap everyone's spear and offer a few monosyllabic utterances.

When the leaders had returned to their respective lineups, Ashby and Clark were left staring across the battleground.

"Ashby, you have a choice," Clark said. "Go back to the VITRIOL or die. Take the hunters away from the village or die. It's as simple as that."

"These are husbands and wives, Colonel Clark. You can't simply send the men out wandering."

"Ashby – look at you, dragging these poor men into *folly* because of the guilt you feel. You abandoned your family for your career – for this – and now you want to make *me* feel bad about doing what I want for myself and what I believe will advance this civilization in the same way we were advanced millions of years ago when aliens landed on *our own* planet."

"What the hell are you talking about?"

"Ashby, go back to the ship. Or I will kill you. Do you understand?"

"Colonel Clark, not only have you lost your mind, but you've sunken into a state of self-absorbtion that has ruined – completely *ruined* – a multi-million-dollar government experiment. Your happiness means *squat* to me, or them, and it is *you* my friend who are about to die at the hands of the very creatures you tried to find your happiness with."

"I will kill you… with my bare hands."

A whooshing sound, like bird wings, passed with a dust cloud. Everyone turned to the gigantic rock, where a redheaded woman had appeared in a ceremonial Cleopatra costume, swinging slings in each hand.

liii.

Clark aimed his field binoculars.

The woman walked steadily, gracefully, without even a stray glance, as if in her own blind commencement. She wore a crown with gold horns, adorned with lunar and solar symbols and two purple plumes. Her open-backed dress was made of feather-like gold lamé, tight on her curvy figure, her forearms lined with gold bracelets. Like a baton twirler in a parade, marching in sync with her spinning slings, she made a beeline for the spaceship.

She stopped beneath the VITRIOL. Half a dozen vultures, perched on the funnel, looked down upon her. She slowed her left hand and intensified the right, releasing a gray stone that grazed a bird's wing. It squawked and shifted, but continued to stare down at the woman. She released the other, hitting a bird squarely in the head. It dropped over the edge and struggled, falling, before taking wing and gliding down to the ground. She picked up another stone and repeated, swinging the sling so hard it became a blur, hitting a bird in the chest. It screeched and shot up like a demon, then swooped and landed at a safe distance.

Three birds remained. She knelt down, keeping her knees together, and grabbed a few more stones. But before she could pack the slings, a sharp hiss passed over the sky. The slings fell from her hands. Her body nearly levitated in pain, her chest surging and her shoulder blades back. She dropped to her knees, gazing up at the spaceship as she collapsed.

liv.

A breeze scattered the last layer of cloud to reveal the brown contours of the cliffs. Light elevated everything: the muddy colors of the village, the coarse thatch and tanned animal skins sagging with bits of bone and teeth and stubble, and the ghostly pall of everyone's skin.

Another wind followed, almost a sigh. It hovered and vanished, leaving no drift, no movement, nothing; while all eyes remained on the beautifully dressed woman facedown with the beaded arrow in her back.

A deep, beastly moan came from above. Everyone turned to see, on the western precipice, a slouching shadow: a wooly mammoth ridden by a lone figure.

lv.

Clark aimed his field binoculars at the promontory.

The man riding the mammoth had yellow-brown skin -- darker than the Uhluk -- and long jet-black hair. He wore an embroidered shirt, made of patches of animal hide, symmetrical rows of stringed beads and long tassels of what appeared to be human hair. Below, he wore a breechcloth and a pair of ankle-high leather boots with a tight front stitch. A quiver and bow stuck out behind his shoulders.

Another man – wearing a similar shirt – rolled a body with his foot, pushing it over the edge. It bounced like a pinball down the choppy slope and hit the ground hard, facing up.

Clark ran toward the body.

"Colonel, stop," Ashby said.

Clark focused the zoom. It was a man in U.S. Army fatigues. He'd been scalped.

"What do you see, Colonel?"

He aimed back up at the promontory. The dark-haired men stared down at them.

"Talk to me, Colonel."

"We've been tricked, Sir."

"What did you see, Colonel Clark? Give me the field glasses."

Ashby adjusted the lenses and aimed up at the promontory.

"We've been set up," Clark said.

Ashby aimed at the military man on the ground.

Clark continued, breathless. "This is why I was concerned… when I… when we…" he turned to one of the hunters "this is why I asked the Planet Watcher those questions." The hunter smiled and nodded while the rest watched bug-eyed.

Ashby lowered the field glasses. "Get a hold of yourself, Colonel."

Clark grabbed Ashby's arm. "Colonel, I had a feeling from the very beginning, way back in training. *This* is why during our U Maj 47D briefing I asked about colonization! See? I'm not crazy."

"What are you saying?"

"What I'm saying is…." Clark looked across the Uhluk natives, whose mouths were all hanging open. "What I'm saying, Sir, is that this planet here…" Clark kicked the ground.

"Spit it out, Clark."

'Sir, *this planet has already been colonized by the U.S. Government.*"

"Look, I just… What?"

"NASA sent us here for some unknown purpose – to interact with this underdeveloped tribe, to settle a dispute between the Uhluk here and that advanced one up there – I have no idea. But now we're now stuck in the middle of an intergalactic skirmish and in danger of being killed. Or mutilated like that Army guy."

Ashby aimed the field glasses again. The man standing beside the mammoth held a lance decorated with beads and feathers. He stepped back and the lance soared like a flare across the sky, falling fifty feet in front of them, sticking perfectly in the ground.

lvi.

For some reason, Francine was stuck on *Time Bandits*, in particular the scene when the midgets are walking across the desert and hit that invisible wall, their little cheeks and noses pressing against the glass. Of course there were more pressing things to think about -- like Sharise's outlandish showgirl get-up and the cheap-looking arrow special effect, not to mention the mannequin in camouflage that got tossed over the cliff – but the most pressing, of course, was the decision of how to *react* to these occurrences.

Which brought her to *Don't Look Now*. Not the serpentine sex scene with Julie Christie, but near the end when Donald Sutherland is chasing the little red-hooded girl through the canals of Venice, into that misty, abandoned building with the beautiful wainscoting where he finds her crying in the attic, with her face to the wall, and he whispers *va bene, don't worry, I'm a friend* and she turns around and by God it's not a girl at all but a...

And it all made perfect sense.

lvii.

The silence was broken by the mammoth rider, who wailed and pointed at the Jarlsburg Butte, above which – on the cliff's edge – a throng of several dozen dark-haired people appeared with a long roll, like a rug, over their heads. They unfurled it over the edge, revealing an enormous blood-red patchwork. With a resounding clap it fell onto the Jarlsburg Butte, covering it completely and rolling out a cloud of dust.

Around the entire circumference of the valley rim rose an army of these figures. They bore feather lances, longbows and beaded arrows, shields and hatchets, and buffered the air with the flabby pounding of a drum.

<u>A Few Reasons Why You Should Visit BUFFALO BILL'S WILD WEST:</u>

1st – Because it is a LIVING PICTURE OF LIFE ON THE FRONTIER
2nd – You will see INDIANS, COWBOYS, and MEXICANS as they live
3rd – You will see BUFFALO, ELK, WILD HORSES, and a multitude of curiosities
4th – You will see a BUFFALO HUNT in ALL ITS REALISTIC DETAILS

11th – You will see an authentic MEEMAW VILLAGE, transplanted from the Plains
12th – You will see the secrets of MEEMAW trackers and scouts
13th – You will see vicious MEEMAW WARFARE depicted in true colors

– From the original 1890 Show Program for Buffalo Bill's Wild West Show; courtesy of the Duluth Sideshow Museum, Duluth, Minn.

lviii.

"What's your order, Colonel?"

Ashby tossed the field glasses to Erasmus Clark. "That's a sophisticated tribe up there."

"Must be a thousand of them."

Ashby counted the Uhluk. "Best get all these people into the VITRIOL."

"Are you kidding?"

"We have extra belted pods in the hold. If we can't launch safely, we'll scare them away with the reactor boosters."

"You mean launch these natives into space?"

"Better than leaving them to die."

"I guess." Clark looked around at the natives, whose hangdog expressions were worse than ever. "Come on everyone, come on!" he waved, walking toward the spaceship. Someone grabbed his arm, and he turned to see Luhk.

Her expression was heavy, but resolved and determined. Even amid all this danger, he couldn't help but think of her body. Already he knew every inch of it, and somewhere in a far-flung corner of his brain he was eternally caressing it, tasting it and making it cringe like an animal.

She unhooked his TASER sheath and put the gun in his hand. She took a breath and said, "R-r-r-r-r…"

"Yes?" He had never heard this tone before.

"R-r-r-e-p-e-a-t-ed."

"Yes?" he said aghast, looking around at the natives, who were equally stunned.

"D-d… D-i-s-p-l-a-y-s…."

"My god…"

"O-o-f… of…"

"Yes?"

"D-d-d… D-o-m-i-n-a-n-c-e."

Clark took a breath that nearly made him float. He released the stun gun safety and got down on his knees.

By the end of Francine's utterance, everyone had realized exactly how this particular moment should be *experienced*. Turning away from reason, they found themselves brutally awash in the understanding that all experience converged at this callous epiphany; that life, at the very end, is held together by simple fibers; you lived happily or suffered, you took or had taken, you killed or were killed. And they all felt the resulting calm.

Francine ran the warrior line, anointing their weapons with the might of the Uhluk Tribe, and leading everyone around the outside of the thatched village to the surface road, where an unending file of bow-strung warriors marched; a seething and ferocious and hot-blooded contingent of the sanguinary Meemaw Nation.

THE END

Printed in the United States
71716LV00001BB/10-18

9 780977 376339